United States Department of Agriculture
Forest Service

Pacific Southwest
Research Station

Research Paper
PSW-RP-265

September 2013

Pinus ponderosa: Geographic Races and Subspecies Based on Morphological Variation

Robert Z. Callaham

Author

Robert Z. Callaham (retired) was a botanist, geneticist with the Pacific Southwest Research Station, 800 Buchanan Street, West Annex Building, Albany, CA 94710-0011. He served as station director from 1976 to 1983 and as de facto director (1983 to 1990), Wildland Resources Center, University of California. He can be reached at: rzcallaham@comcast.net.

Cover photograph: Chris Evans, Illinois Wildlife Action Plan Bugwood org.

Abstract

Callaham, Robert Z. 2013. *Pinus ponderosa*: geographic races and subspecies based on morphological variation. Res. Pap. PSW-RP-265. Albany, CA: U.S. Department of Agriculture, Forest Service, Pacific Southwest Research Station. 53 p.

Morphological variation of ponderosa pine (*Pinus ponderosa* Dougl. ex Laws.), growing north of Mexico, is described. A map shows distributions of five putative races that are analyzed and discussed. Characteristics of branches, shoots, and needles were measured for 10 or fewer trees growing on 147 plots located at 1,500-ft elevational intervals along latitudinal transects. Characteristics of cones were measured from 120 of these plots. Cones from 78 plots yielded seeds for study. Subspecific boundaries were based on both visual interpretations for many traits and statistical cluster analyses of plot means. Boundaries were tested for appropriateness by multiple discriminant analyses. Univariate analyses of variance and stepwise discriminant analyses selected characteristics most capable of differentiating among hypothesized races. On average, 98 percent of plots were correctly classified as to race. Characteristics most capable of differentiating among the hypothesized races were selected. Characteristics of trees in three common-garden plantings were analyzed to determine the genetic basis of foliar characteristics measured on trees in situ. Results of analyses and review of literature confirm existence of five morphologically distinct, geographic taxa and four transition zones.

Keywords: Ponderosa pine, geographic races, morphological variation.

Contents

Introduction

Ponderosa pine (*Pinus ponderosa* Dougl. ex Laws.) is the most prevalent and valuable conifer in the western United States. It is estimated to cover 33.7 million ac in 16 Western States plus additional areas in adjacent British Columbia. Perry (1991) affirmed that it does not occur in Mexico, but this contention needs to be further validated by studies of pines growing in northern Mexico. Ponderosa pine occurs in eight of 23 major forest cover types in the western United States (Burns 1983). Across its vast geographic range, the species varies considerably in morphology, ecology, and habits of growth. Its patterns of inherent variation have been studied since 1925 at the U.S. Depatment of Agriculture Forest Service's Institute of Forest Genetics (IFG), Pacific Southwest Research Station, Placerville, California.

In 1954, the author, then a geneticist at IFG, began comprehensive investigations of ponderosa pine from its range north of Mexico. The objective was to define the nature and extent of intraspecific variability. Several studies were conducted to establish inherent similarities and differences of trees growing in the United States and Canada (Callaham 1959, 1961, 1962). Reported here is the study of morphological variability of trees growing in situ.

Few investigators had scrutinized in situ variation in morphology of a widespread tree species to the extent done in this study. Critchfield's (1957) comprehensive investigation of lodgepole pine (*P. contorta* Dougl. ex Loud.) throughout its range inspired this study and served as its model.

Literature Review

Taxonomically, ponderosa pine has long been recognized as being composed of three varieties. Little (1979) recognized:

(1) *Pinus ponderosa* Dougl. ex C. Lawson var. *ponderosa* as typical ponderosa pine because the species was originally described from a collection near Spokane, Washington, extending southward from British Columbia, west of the Continental Divide, into Idaho, Washington, Oregon, and northeastern California.

(2) Rocky Mountain ponderosa pine, *P. ponderosa* var. *scopulorum* Engelm. (1880), elevated to a subspecies by E. Murray (1982), occurring in Montana and Wyoming, east of the Continental Divide, and extending southward through Utah, Colorado, and Nebraska into Arizona, New Mexico, the Oklahoma panhandle (upper Tessequite Canyon in western Cimarron County),[1] western Texas, and Mexico.

---

[1] Oklahoma Biological Survey, http://www.biosurvey.ou.edu/shrub/pipo htm. (2013).

(3) Arizona pine, *P. ponderosa* var. *arizonica* (Engelm.) Shaw, a five-needled form having elongated, curving, semipersistent cones, growing in extreme southwestern New Mexico, southeastern Arizona, and adjacent northern Mexico.

The first two taxa were expected to be refined as a result of the investigation undertaken in this study.

Most investigators have studied variation within pines by growing progenies of diverse provenances in one or more common gardens (a uniform plantation of trees at a geographic location) (Callaham 1964). So-called provenance studies of ponderosa pine began in 1913 and have been reported by many authors (see Conkle and Critchfield 1988). Wells (1964a) and Read (1980, 1983) comprehensively reviewed results of provenance studies of ponderosa pine. Both also presented their views on geographic races based on seedling progenies grown in nurseries.

Wells used seed from 60 of the provenance collections reported here, and Read's seed collections were from 80 provenances mostly east of the Continental Divide. Wells (1964b) determined correlations between characteristics of seedlings, grown in a provenance study in Michigan, and Callaham's range-wide climatic data.

Rehfeldt (1986a, 1986b, 1990, 1991, 1993) conducted a series of provenance studies to determine patterns of genetic variation in a broad north-south band extending from the border with Canada almost to the border with Mexico. Sorenson (1994) used Rehfeldt's approach in a provenance study in Oregon east of the Cascade Range.

Only two authors have studied in situ variation across the range of ponderosa pine. Haller (1965) studied occurrence of two-needled fascicles and proposed racial boundaries for ponderosa pine based on geographic distribution of two-needled fascicles, mean annual precipitation, and mean minimum temperatures in January. Haller's boundaries coincided closely with those of races drawn earlier by Weidman (1939) (fig. 1).

Smith (1977), after studying monoterpenes from xylem oleoresin at 68 locations, divided ponderosa pine into five regional types with four transitional zones. Except for combining regions in the north and designating some new regions in southern California and Arizona, his boundaries are synonymous with Haller's. Sturgeon (1979) refined Smith's boundary between races in northern California and southern Oregon.

Critchfield (1984) established both close identity of Washoe pine (*Pinus washoensis* H. Mason and Stockwell) (1945) with Weidman's "North Plateau ponderosa pine" and extent of significant barriers to crossing among three races of ponderosa

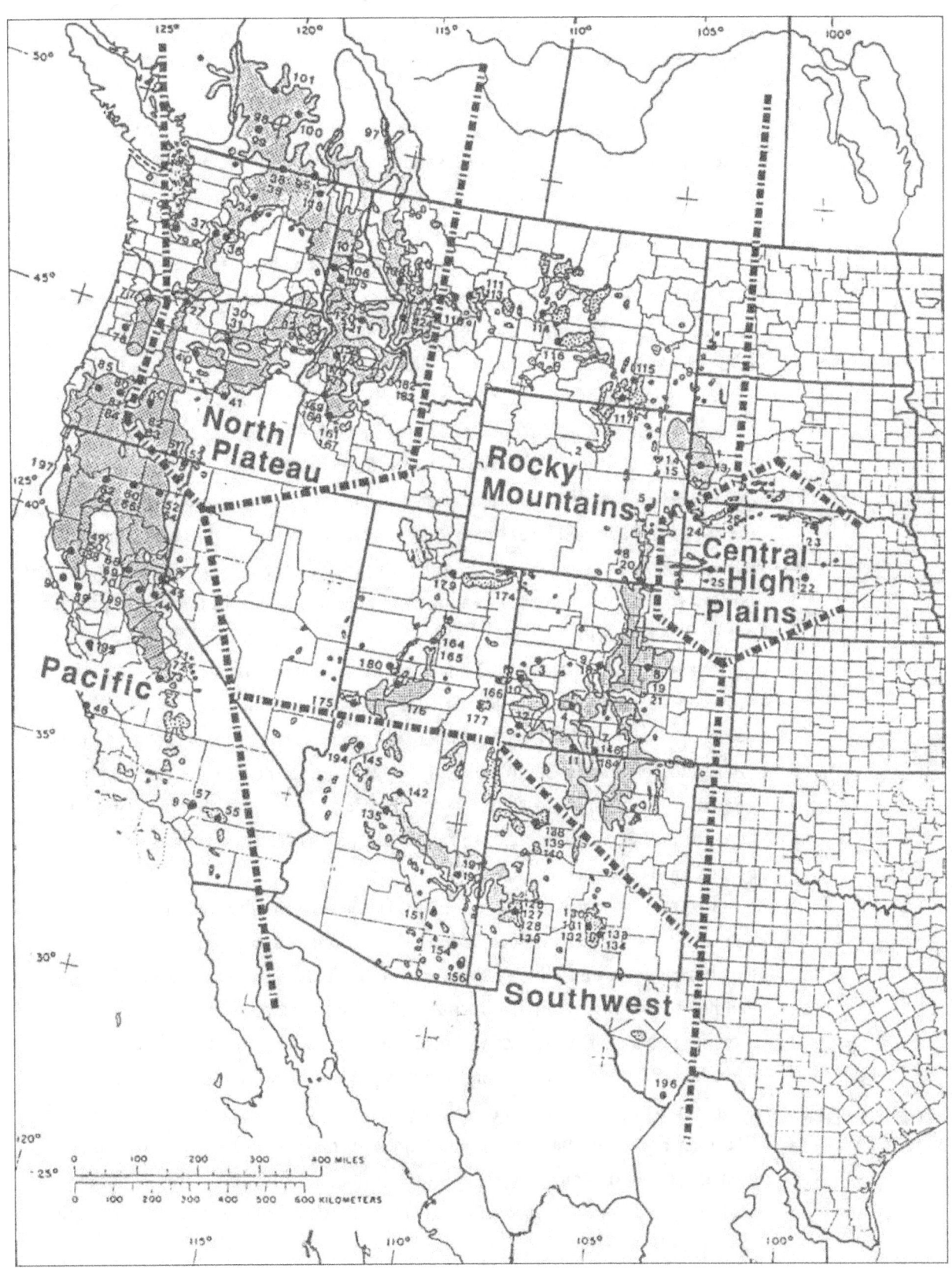

Figure 1—Distribution of ponderosa pine and plots established for this study with tentative boundaries between races used for analyses of data.

pine. He concluded: "There are partial reproductive barriers between the Pacific and Rocky Mountains races and likely barriers between Pacific and North Plateau races."

Critchfield's scholarly review of this situation and his personal knowledge of genetics and geography of ponderosa pine resulted in his boundaries and transition regions among geographic races being drawn much as is done in this report.

Linhart et al. (1989) were first to publish data on differences in allozymes—allelic variants of genes that determine enzymes detected using electrophoresis—associated with races of ponderosa pine. Their work involved only 15 individuals of the Pacific race (from five plots closely clustered at low elevation on the west slope of the Sierra Nevada) and five individuals of the Rocky Mountains race (two each from Nebraska and Wyoming and one from South Dakota). Their findings "suggest ... there are significant differences between *ponderosa* and *scopulorum* varieties." Niebling and Conkle (1990) studied variation in allozymes and reported: "Major differences existed between the Rocky Mountain(s) race of ponderosa pine and ... the Pacific race of ponderosa pine (actually trees growing at two locations in the transitional zone between Pacific and North Plateau races), and North Plateau race ponderosa pine." Differences in allozymes among all races of ponderosa pine have not yet been assessed.

Grant et al. (1989) studied 14 morphological characters of 3-year-old seedlings grown in a greenhouse in Colorado from intravarietal and intervarietal crosses. Female parents grew near Placerville, California. Male parents grew near Placerville and in Nebraska, South Dakota, and Wyoming. They concluded: "Intravarietal progeny were distinctly differentiated genetically from intervarietal sibships in seven of fourteen characters examined." They also estimated narrow-sense heritabilities for the 14 characters.

Monson and Grant (1989), using two of the seedling families studied by Grant and coworkers (1989), established heritable differences in physiological traits. Particularly relevant to this study of morphological variation was their discovery that ponderosa pines from California differed significantly from ponderosa pines growing in Niobrara County, Wyoming, in stomata per square millimeter, stomata per millimeter along one row, and stomata per millimeter of needle width. When compared with an interracial (California x Wyoming) hybrid family, the intraracial (California x California) family had "higher stomatal densities ... expressed in a greater number of stomatal rows per unit of needle width and a greater number of stomata per unit of needle length ... sizes of the stomatal openings ... were not significantly different."

Rehfeldt demonstrated the existence of clinal patterns of genetic variability in races of ponderosa pine. His studies covered provenances growing in a broad band (the land measured 217 mi across northeastern Washington to the Continental Divide and 416 mi across Utah, Colorado, Arizona, and New Mexico) extending from Canada to Mexico. In a series of parallel studies, he examined growth, shoot elongation, and damage during winter of seedlings in common gardens and in a greenhouse. For these studies, Rehfeldt collected seed-bearing cones from 353 populations: 201 in Columbia basins (1986a, 1986b, 1991), 56 + 16 in Utah and Colorado, respectively (1990, 1993), and 78 in Arizona and New Mexico (1993). His purposes were to explain patterns of genetic variation and to provide guidance for transfer of seeds to reduce maladaptations in reforestation. Through multiple regression analyses, he demonstrated existence of complex clinal patterns of variation and their parallels to patterns of environmental variation—particularly topography, precipitation, and length of frost-free season. He did not study characteristics of parent trees from which he collected cones and seeds, so a great potential for understanding in situ variability in ponderosa pine from a broad north-south transect was not realized.

Wells (1964a, 1964b) reported characteristics of his seedling progenies grown in a nursery in Michigan from seed collected for the study reported here. His study of seedlings essentially was a common garden planting. The study reported here describes in situ attributes of some of his parent trees.

Little's (1979) third taxon, Arizona pine, was specifically excluded from this study. Investigations at the IFG, Placerville, California, had already established that *P. arizonica* Engelm. was a species. Later, Peloquin (1984) and Rehfeldt (1993) confirmed the distinctness of Arizona pine.

This report purposely refers either to the two, long-recognized varieties of the species or to five races of ponderosa pine (fig. 1). These races are morphologically distinct geographic variants within the species.

Collections

In late summer 1955, nearly 200 foresters working on national forests, for state agencies, and for private industry were asked to establish tagged-tree plots and to collect specified materials. Because instructions and materials were posted to designated collectors, these immediately were named "mail order" collections. Collectors were asked to provide data describing sampled trees and collection localities (plots) and samples of cones, shoots, needles, bark, and wood. By return mail, they provided data sheets and specimens from 147 plots, cones from 120 plots, and viable seeds from 78 plots (table 1).

Table 1—Locations of plots from which data were available

Plot	North latitude	West longitude	Elevation	State or province	Weather station
			Feet		
1	43°57'	103°36'	5,400	South Dakota	Deerfield Dam/Custer
2	44°03'	107°18'	6,300	Wyoming	Tensleep
3	38°58'	108°06'	7,300	Colorado	Cedaredge
4	38°15'	106°42'	9,000	Colorado	Cotchetopa/Cathedral
5	42°27'	105°28'	6,400	Wyoming	Double-4 Ranch
6	39°00'	104°46'	7,100	Colorado	Husted
7	37°04'	106°15'	8,600	Colorado	San Antone R.S./Chama, New Mexico
8	40°58'	105°27'	7,700	Colorado	St. Cloud/Fry's Ranch
9	39°02'	106°15'	9,000	Colorado	Twin Lakes/Buena Vista
10	37°28'	108°29'	7,500	Colorado	Fort Lewis
11	37°10'	107°00'	7,500	Colorado	Pagosa Springs
12	37°31'	108°29'	7,500	Colorado	Fort Lewis
13	44°03'	103°37'	5,500	South Dakota	Deerfield Dam/Custer
14	43°54'	104°03'	6,200	South Dakota	Boyd/Newcastle, Wyoming
15	43°53'	104°02'	6,200	South Dakota	Boyd/Newcastle, Wyoming
18	38°57'	105°59'	9,200	Colorado	Hartsell/Cripple Creek
19	38°54'	104°57'	7,200	Colorado	Monument
20	41°00'	105°29'	6,900	Colorado	Box Elder/Fry's Ranch
21	39°00'	105°00'	9,100	Colorado	Monument
22	41°28'	100°01'	2,800	Nebraska	Stapleton
23	42°45'	99°32'	2,100	Nebraska	Newport
24	42°44'	103°48'	4,500	Nebraska	Harrison
25	41°26'	103°05'	4,200	Nebraska	Dalton/Sidney
26	43°04'	102°38'	3,000	South Dakota	Pine Ridge
27	45°41'	121°21'	200	Oregon	Hood River
30	44°55'	119°41'	3,200	Oregon	Loverock and Ukiah1NE
31	44°59'	119°45'	4,500	Oregon	Loverock and Ukiah1NE
32	45°00'	118°06'	4,500	Oregon	Austin
33	45°00'	117°00'	4,600	Oregon	Gumboot/Sparta
34	47°58'	120°18'	2,200	Washington	Lakeside
36	46°56'	120°32'	1,600	Washington	Ellensberg
37	46°58'	120°51'	4,600	Washington	Ellensberg
38	48°58'	119°23'	1,600	Washington	Oroville
39	48°55'	119°17'	3,000	Washington	Chesaw
40	44°16'	120°26'	5,000	Oregon	Ochoco R.S.
41	43°49'	119°18'	4,700	Oregon	Bear Creek/Seneca
44	38°48'	120°09'	6,000	California	Woodfords
45	39°14'	119°56'	6,500	Nevada	Glenbrook
46	36°13'	121°43'	3,000	California	Big Sur State Park/Priest Valley

Table 1—Locations of plots from which data were available (continued)

Plot	North latitude	West longitude	Elevation	State or province	Weather station
			Feet		
49	39°09'	122°47'	4,400	California	Clearlake Park
50	39°07'	122°45'	2,800	California	Clearlake Park
51	41°57'	120°46'	5,400	California	Lakeview, Oregon
52	41°05'	120°55'	4,700	California	Adin R.S./Madeline
53	41°54'	120°19'	6,000	California	Fort Bidwell
54	41°00'	120°55'	5,800	California	Blacks Mtn Branch/ Madeline
55	34°10'	116°56'	6,000	California	Seven Oaks
57	34°14'	117°14'	6,000	California	Lake Arrowhead
60	41°04'	121°35'	4,600	California	Fall River Mills Intake
62	40°59'	122°26'	1,600	California	Vollmers/Weaverville R.S.
64	40°59'	122°32'	4,400	California	Weaverville R.S.
66	40°59'	121°35'	3,100	California	Hat Creek P.H. No.1
68	39°01'	120°49'	3,200	California	Foresthill R.S./Gold Run
69	38°56'	121°00'	1,500	California	Auburn
70	39°05'	120°45'	4,500	California	Blue Canyon
71	37°05'	119°17'	4,500	California	Big Creek P.H. No.1
72	37°04'	119°15'	3,200	California	Auberry
73	37°02'	119°07'	6,100	California	Huntington Lake
77	45°29'	122°52'	200	Oregon	Portland
78	44°27'	123°18'	300	Oregon	Corvallis
79	47°02'	122°32'	300	Washington	McMillin Reservoir
80	42°59'	122°31'	4,300	Oregon	Prospect
81	42°59'	122°52'	1,400	Oregon	Riddle
82	43°00'	121°48'	4,500	Oregon	Chemult
83	42°59'	121°57'	5,900	Oregon	Crater Lake
84	43°00'	122°45'	3,150	Oregon	Prospect
85	42°58'	123°35'	1,450	Oregon	Glendale
88	38°50'	122°42'	3,100	California	Hobergs/Lakeport
89	38°23'	122°31'	500	California	Santa Rosa
90	38°45'	122°46'	1,400	California	Kellogg/Clear Lake Park
93	44°55'	117°05'	3,000	Oregon	Halfway
94	45°00'	118°05'	5,900	Oregon	Ibex Mine/Baker
95	49°07'	118°25'	3,200	British Columbia	Chesaw, Washington
96	49°05'	115°08'	2,600	British Columbia	Fortine, Montana
97	50°09'	115°53'	3,300	British Columbia	Kimberly
98	49°27'	120°26'	2,000	British Columbia	Princeton
99	49°34'	120°29'	3,300	British Columbia	Manning Park
100	50°12'	119°32'	1,700	British Columbia	V. Coldstream Ranch
101	50°53'	120°13'	2,400	British Columbia	Kamloops

Table 1—Locations of plots from which data were available (continued)

Plot	North latitude	West longitude	Elevation	State or province	Weather station
			Feet		
102	48°56'	116°25'	1,800	Idaho	Porthill
105	46°59'	116°14'	3,800	Idaho	St. Maries
106	46°59'	116°49'	3,000	Idaho	Potlach
107	47°01'	116°15'	3,000	Idaho	Deary/St. Maries
108	47°00'	114°41'	2,900	Montana	Superior
109	46°59'	114°43'	4,600	Montana	Superior
110	46°57'	112°38'	4,400	Montana	Ovando
111	47°02'	112°10'	4,500	Montana	Ovando
113	47°06'	112°15'	6,000	Montana	Adel
114	46°59'	109°29'	4,500	Montana	Lewiston
115	45°39'	104°09'	4,100	Montana	Rocky Point, Wyoming
116	46°15'	108°28'	4,500	Montana	Rapelje 45
117	45°13'	106°16'	4,300	Montana	Ashland
118	48°46'	118°07'	1,400	Washington	Northport
119	46°09'	115°45'	1,500	Idaho	Kooskia
120	46°00'	115°55'	3,100	Idaho	Grangeville
121	45°53'	115°58'	4,400	Idaho	Grangeville
123	46°05'	114°11'	4,200	Montana	Darby
124	46°05'	114°14'	4,500	Montana	Darby
125	46°06'	114°17'	5,800	Montana	Darby
126	32°53'	107°55'	7,500	New Mexico	Mimbres R.S./Fort Bayard
127	32°57'	107°51'	9,000	New Mexico	Mimbres R.S./Fort Bayard
128	32°51'	107°57'	6,100	New Mexico	Mimbres R.S./Fort Bayard
129	33°10'	107°45'	7,300	New Mexico	Hermosa
130	32°58'	105°50'	7,200	New Mexico	Mountain Park
131	33°00'	105°47'	8,000	New Mexico	Cloudcroft
132	33°00'	105°42'	9,000	New Mexico	Cloudcroft
133	32°54'	105°29'	6,000	New Mexico	Mayhill R.S.
134	32°56'	105°35'	7,500	New Mexico	Mayhill R.S.
135	34°55'	112°59'	7,200	Arizona	Walnut Creek/Prescott
138	35°13'	107°43'	7,500	New Mexico	Marquez/Grants
139	35°16'	107°38'	9,000	New Mexico	Marquez/Grants
140	35°15'	107°34'	10,300	New Mexico	Marquez/Grants
142	35°08'	111°49'	7,300	Arizona	Flagstaff
145	36°23'	113°10'	7,300	Arizona	Tuweep/Fredonia

Table 1—Locations of plots from which data were available (continued)

Plot	North latitude	West longitude	Elevation	State or province	Weather station
			Feet		
146	36°58'	106°09'	9,000	New Mexico	San Antone R.S./Chama
151	33°18'	110°50'	7,400	Arizona	Globe
154	32°40'	109°52'	9,100	Arizona	Fort Grant/Wilcox
156	31°51'	109°14'	8,525	Arizona	Portal
158	44°52'	116°30'	4,900	Idaho	McCall
159	44°14'	116°09'	4,200	Idaho	Alpha 1NE
160	44°51'	116°30'	3,900	Idaho	Mew Meadows R.S.
161	43°52'	115°50'	4,500	Idaho	Idaho City
164	38°59'	111°22'	8,200	Utah	Ephraim Hq., GBRC/Emery
165	39°00'	111°19'	8,200	Utah	Ephraim Hq., GBRC/Emery
166	38°25'	109°08'	8,900	Utah	LaSal
167	43°43'	115°52'	4,500	Idaho	Idaho City
168	43°54'	116°00'	6,000	Idaho	Idaho City
170	44°54'	115°43'	4,500	Idaho	Big Creek 1S
171	44°53'	115°40'	6,000	Idaho	Big Creek 1S
173	44°57'	114°37'	6,000	Idaho	Big Creek 1S
174	40°53'	109°38'	7,600	Utah	Manila
175	37°23'	113°30'	6,800	Utah	Pine Valley/Cedar City
176	37°45'	112°39'	8,700	Utah	Panguich
177	37°41'	109°49'	8,400	Utah	Monticello
179	40°38'	111°10'	7,500	Utah	Park City
180	38°15'	112°28'	7,500	Utah	Beaver Canyon P.H./Beaver
182	45°33'	113°57'	4,700	Idaho	Salmon
183	45°32'	114°04'	5,800	Idaho	Salmon
184	36°59'	106°59'	6,200	New Mexico	Dulce
190	33°58'	109°48'	9,000	Arizona	McNary
191	34°03'	109°42'	7,500	Arizona	McNary
193	36°47'	113°45'	6,900	Arizona	MountTrumbull/Grand Canyon
194	36°07'	113°48'	6,100	Arizona	Mount Trumbull/Grand Canyon
195	37°20'	121°39'	4,000	California	Mount Hamilton
196	29°17'	103°15'	6,000	Texas	Chisos Basin
197	40°58'	123°41'	1,700	California	China Flat
198	37°03'	122°08'	1,600	California	Ben Lomand
199	38°44'	120°44'	2,700	California	Placerville

R.S. = ranger station, P.H. = power house, INE and IS = weather service designations, GBRC = Great Basin Research Center.

Insofar as possible, plots were located within 5 mi north and south of the odd degrees of latitude from 29° to 51° north latitude. This provided a spacing of approximately 130 mi north and south between collections. Thus, each of five races identified by study of literature were sampled along three to five latitudinal transects (fig. 1). Where transects missed large portions of the range, subsidiary collections were made.

Along latitudinal transects, plots were established at elevational intervals of approximately 1,500 ft. Plots were located so as to provide two or three collections on each side of major north-south mountain ranges. Elevations of established plots ranged from 200 ft in Oregon to 10,300 ft in New Mexico. Insofar as possible, plots were located within 200 vertical ft of prescribed elevations: 1,500, 3,000, 4,500 ft, *et seq.*

The collector establishing a plot recorded exact location and elevation and described topography, soil, and stand conditions and identified each tree with a numbered tag. Plots were located in stands of natural origin containing at least 10 cone-bearing trees, each separated from the others by a minimum of 100 ft.

The 10 trees selected for collection on each plot were to be of average form, growth rate, and branch habit. Conspicuously crooked, slow-growing, or thick-branched trees were to be avoided. Preference was to be given to thrifty young trees. Cones on selected trees were to be ripe, as evidenced by a browning in color and opening of basal scales, but many less-than-fully-ripe cones were collected.

Four characteristics of each selected tree were recorded in the field:

(1) Average number of years that needles remained green (C1)[2] was estimated from an examination of four thrifty branches that could be reached from the ground.

(2) Average distance (inches) from tip of branch to oldest green needles (C2) was estimated from measurements of the four branches.

(3) After counting the branches in the top five whorls, the collector estimated the average number of branches per whorl (C3). (Ponderosa pine usually produces only one whorl each year.)

(4) The angle branches at the tree's apex made with the trunk of the tree (C4) was sketched by the collector and subsequently was measured in the laboratory with a protractor to the nearest 10 degrees.

Materials sampled from each selected tree included fascicles of needles, two vigorous shoots, five cones, a standard increment core, and a piece of bark. A

---

[2] Characteristics used in this study are described here and henceforth are designated C1 *et seq.* See table 2 for complete list.

fascicle of needles was picked from the center of each annual cluster of fascicles on each of the four thrifty branches measured for traits C1 and C2. Thus, if green needles were retained 3 years, then 12 fascicles were collected. These materials—with the plot description and a map showing the location—were mailed to IFG. All materials collected, after processing, were deposited in IFG's herbarium. The bark samples were mounted for study, but differences in color or other characteristics were not apparent. Increment cores were not used but are archived at IFG.

Note that during 1955, ripening cones were found primarily on plots in the eastern part of the range of ponderosa pine. During 1956, a second attempt was made to collect ripe cones from remaining plots. Collectors were asked, in the event of failure of the cone crop, to take five cones from the ground beneath sample trees or nearby trees. Ultimately, cones were collected from 120 plots, but seeds were available from only 78 plots.

Trees growing in three common garden plantations in Oregon and Washington were studied to estimate heritability of characteristics. Observations were made in these plantations early in 1956, and materials were collected for measurements in the laboratory. Each plantation contained one 16-tree block planting of progenies from 10 widely separated provenances of ponderosa pine from the:

- Pacific race: Steilacoom (Washington), Willamette (Oregon), and Eldorado (California)
- Transition between the Pacific and North Plateau races: Rogue River (Oregon) and Lassen (California)
- North Plateau race: Bitterroot (Montana) and Deschutes (Oregon)
- Rocky Mountains race: Harney (Black Hills, South Dakota)
- Southwestern race: Coconino (Arizona) and Carson (New Mexico).

These plantations were established in 1928 and 1929 with 2-0 stock grown from seed collected in seven states (Squillace and Silen 1962). For this study one 16-tree, square plot was established for each of 10 provenance at each of three planting sites:

(1) Oregon State University's McDonald Forest near Corvallis at 950 ft elevation (near native Pacific-race ponderosa pines)

(2) U.S. Forest Service's Wind River Experimental Forest near Carson, Washington, at 1,300 ft elevation

(3) Deschutes National Forest near Bend, Oregon, at 4,200 ft elevation (among native North Plateau-race ponderosa pines)

None of these trees provided cones or seeds.

Foliage, Cones, and Seed

Materials were received at Placerville and processed a few days after collection. Shoot specimens were placed in a conventional plant press after hue (C5), value (C6), and chroma (C7) of foliage color had been estimated using Munsell Color Charts.[3] Ten fascicles of needles were randomly selected and measured (C8). Lengths of 10 randomly selected needles produced in 1955 were measured. That length was expressed as multiples of length of primary bracts comprising the still-papery sheath surrounding the base of each fascicle. An average for this ratio—needle length/sheath length (C9)—was calculated. The number of needles per fascicle (C10) was determined.

From the middle of one needle in each of the 10 randomly chosen fascicles, a short section was removed and prepared for microscopic examination. Thickness of needles (actually radius of the fascicle, C11) was measured. Semicircles from two-needled fascicles and pie-shaped sections from three-needled fascicles were the subjects measured (in units of an optical micrometer). Each needle of ponderosa pine has two large resin ducts, one in each outside corner. Other smaller resin ducts were counted on adaxial and abaxial sides of each needle. Average numbers of adaxial (C12) and abaxial (C13) resin ducts were calculated. The average number of thick-walled hypodermal cell layers (immediately inside the epidermis) in corners of needles (C14) was determined.

Length and breadth of each of up to five dried cones from a tree were measured. Averages of length of cones (C15), width of cones (C16), and cone form (width divided by length) (C17) were calculated for each parent tree.

Calipers were used to measure length of seed plus wing, wing alone, and length and width of each of 10 seeds from each tree. Averages were calculated for seed length (C18), seed width (C19), length of seed plus wing (C20), seed form (length/width) (C23), and absolute wing length (C24).

Wings attached to seeds varied in shape. Some were widest at midpoint between tip of the seed and tip of the wing. Other wings had their widest point closer to tip of the wing. For each of 10 seeds, the widest point was estimated as proportion of distance from tip of the seed to tip of the wing (i.e., 0.4, widest point closer to seed; 0.7, widest point closer to tip of the wing). The average proportional distance for widest point of wing (C21) was calculated.

---

[3] The use of trade or firm names in this publication is for reader information and does not imply endorsement by the U.S. Department of Agriculture of any product or service.

Estimation of Climate

General data on climate for weather stations within the range of ponderosa pine were used to estimate climatic conditions where trees grew. Climatic summaries published by U.S. Weather Bureau (1954) for each state and provided by the British Columbia Forest Service for that province were used to develop climatic data for the station closest to each plot:

- Average precipitation in inches—
  September through June, total and percentage of annual
  May plus June, total and percentage of annual

- Average annual temperature in degrees Fahrenheit—
  April through June = spring
  July mean
  January mean
  July mean minus January mean

- Growing season—
  Length in days
  Date of start
  Day length at start

Climatic data for each weather station were adjusted—using graphical methods developed by Baker (1944)—for differences in elevation between the weather station and the nearby plot.

Data Analyses (by Diebel)

Diebel (1984; see "Acknowledgments") used a stepwise approach to analyze data. Visual interpretation of data for plots arranged geographically was followed by analyses of variance. Results of these analyses were used in cluster analyses to delineate racial boundaries. Tentative races were analyzed by multivariate and univariate statistical techniques to determine validity of boundaries. Data from the three plantations containing 10 provenances were used to estimate genetic control of characteristics used for discriminating races. Finally, simple correlations among climatic and elevational data and morphological characteristics were investigated.

Step 1: visual data interpretation—
Plot mean and variance for each characteristic were calculated and plotted to determine ranges of variability and to identify where discontinuities occurred across the range of ponderosa pine (table 2).

Table 2—Significance of variation among characteristics of ponderosa pines from varying number of plots throughout the range of the species

Characteristics	Code	F-value[a]	Plots
Years needles remain green	C1	22.4	145
Foliaged length: terminal bud to oldest green needles (cm)	C2	20.5	145
Branches per whorl	C3	27.5	144
Angle of branching from stem (10°)	C4	7.3	145
Hue of needle color	C5	2.1	138
Value of needle color	C6	9.5	138
Chroma of needle color	C7	8.8	138
Needle length (mm)	C8	35.6	143
Needle length/fascicle length	C9	21.3	142
Needles per fascicle	C10	20.9	143
Needle thickness (= fascicle radius)	C11	6.2	143
Adaxial resin canals in needles	C12	4.7	145
Abaxial resin canals in needles	C13	3.3	143
Hypodermal cell layers in corners of needles	C14	10.5	143
Seed cones and seeds:			
Cone length (mm)	C15	16.8	120
Cone width (mm)	C16	11.8	120
Cone form (width/length)	C17	1.2NS	120
Seed length (mm)	C18	16.5	78
Seed width (mm)	C19	12.6	78
Seed wing length (mm)	C20	22.1	77
Position from tip of seed to where seed wing widest	C21	14.2	77
Total smaller resin canals (= C12 + C13)	C22	4.6	143
Seed form (length/width)	C23	3.4	78
Absolute length of seed wing (mm) (= C20 - C18)	C24	10.4	77
Proportional length of seed wing (= C20 / C18)	C25	13.1	78

[a] F-values from a one-way analysis of variance on range-wide data; NS = not significant, $p > 0.05$.

Step 2: analyses of variance—

An elementary one-way analysis of variance used plot means (usually for 10 trees, rarely as few as one tree) for each morphological characteristic (as the dependent variable). These analyses pointed to characteristics most likely to be useful as racial discriminators (table 2). Because of unequal numbers of trees within plots, the general linear model (GLM) program in SAS (Ray 1982) was used.

Step 3: cluster analyses—

Branch and foliage characteristics that differed significantly among plots were subjected to cluster analyses. Plot means were analyzed to determine whether racial boundaries could be delineated. Because cone and seed data were not available for many plots, only characteristics of branching, shoots, and foliage were used. Characteristics C1, C2, C3, C8, C9, C10, and C14 (table 2) were included in cluster analyses. The statistical procedure used was Ward's method (Milligan 1980) as emulated by SAS (Ray 1982).

Step 4: analysis of east-west varieties—
Diebel used stepwise selection procedures (Klecka 1980, as emulated in SAS [Ray 1982] with level for inclusion at 0.05) to isolate those foliar characteristics most capable of discriminating between the Rocky Mountains race and ponderosa pines growing to the west. Following isolation of likely discriminators, data from all plots were subjected to discriminant function analysis (Rao 1973) to classify plots into one race or the other.

Because discriminant function procedures require a priori decisions on boundaries, the boundary line was based on analyses of plot means and cluster analyses and on considerations of data and hypotheses described in the literature. For this analysis, meridian 112.5° West was used to separate eastern and western varieties of ponderosa pine in Montana.

This decision was based on a number of criteria. First, while "natural breaks" for needles per fascicle (C10) and hypodermal cells (C14) occurred at 110° meridian, all other morphological characteristics showed a pattern of continuous variation over that portion of the range. Second, using all plots with foliar data, cluster analysis placed plots 110, 111, and 113 in the Rocky Mountains region, despite the "natural breaks." Third, Read (1980) identified the area between the 110° and 112.5° meridians as a transition zone, and he agreed with Weidman's (1939) identification of the Continental Divide as a boundary between races. Therefore, the Continental Divide in Montana was accepted as the boundary between two varieties and races.

Step 5: analysis of races—
Eastern and western varieties of ponderosa pine, as defined by step 4 above, were further subdivided. Racial boundaries were drawn based on consideration of literature and interpretation of results of cluster analyses in step 3.

Five races of ponderosa pine were defined (fig. 1). Using multivariate techniques described in step 4, Diebel first compared all five races simultaneously (step 5A). Then characteristics of foliage, seeds, and cones were compared between adjacent races (step 5B). Comparisons using 140 plots having foliar data were followed by comparisons using fewer plots that had foliar, seed, and cone data.

Multivariate analyses comparing races were supported by Hoetelling's multivariate t-test (Brown 1977) to detect significant differences among races. A simple univariate Student's t-test was also used to test for differences between races for each discriminant characteristic. To characterize each race, mean and standard error of the mean were calculated for each characteristic (table 3).

Step 6: provenance study of foliar discriminators—
Three provenance studies were analyzed for foliar characteristics. A few of the characteristics measured on trees in situ were not measured in the provenance study. Of those used as discriminators of races in step 5, only distance from terminal bud to oldest green needles (C2) was not recorded. Data were analyzed using a linear model:

$$Y_{ijk} = P/i + SS_j + P_i \times SS_j + error_{ijk}$$

where

Y = trait measured,

P = plantation effect where i = 1, 2, 3, and

SS = seed source (or provenance) effect where j = 1, 2...J (usually 10).

Of particular interest in the analysis were relative strengths of seed source and plantation X seed source interactions for those characteristics used as racial discriminators. Diebel hypothesized that seed source effects would be significant, and genotype-environment interaction would be small. Acceptance of this hypothesis would indicate that races defined in step 5 might indeed be based on genetic affinities.

Variances resulting from plantation, provenance, and interaction were calculated by SAS (Ray 1982) according to Hartley, Rao, and LaMotte (1978). This provided data necessary for evaluating genetic significance of races defined by multivariate analyses.

Step 7: correlation between characteristics, climate, and geography—
Coefficients were calculated to determine significance of correlations between mean values of plots for each of 14 foliage, cone, or seed characteristics, with seven climatic variables and then again with three geographic variables. The 140 correlation coefficients were calculated first using means for all plots for the species, as a whole, and again for plots in each of five races.

Results

Step 1: visual data interpretation—
Visual examination of plot means and variances (tables 2 and 3) led to a conclusion that only two "natural breaks" in values of characteristics occurred at the 110° meridian. All fascicles had three needles (C10) on plots 110, 111, and 113 lying between

Table 3—Means with standard errors of means plus range of plot means [by Diebel] derived from multiple measurements on each of 10 trees growing at a varying number of plot locations for in situ morphological characteristics of five races of *Pinus ponderosa*

Races

Characteristics	Pacific				North Plateau				Rocky Mountains				Southwest				Central High Plains			
	Means	SE	Ranges	Plots	Means	SE	Ranges	Plots	Means	SE	Ranges	Plots	Means	SE	Ranges	Plots	Means	SE	Ranges	Plots
Foliage																				
Years needles remain green	3 9	(0 25,	1 4–6 5)	30	4 7	(0 14,	2 2–7 6)	50	5Y7	(0 28,	3 6–7 9)	23	4 3	(0 18,	2 5–5 9)	24	4 7	(0 18,	4 1–5 0)	5
Foliage length on branch (cm)	25 1	(24,	7 4–52 1)	30	26 2	(2 2,	51–84 6)	50	211	(17,	114–42 9)	23	21 8	(27,	66–53 8)	24	42 2	(67,	25 9–65 0)	5
Needle color hue	34 8	(0 25,	32 3–40 4)	27	34 3	(0 10,	31 5–35 2)	47	343	(0 11,	32 9–35 0)	22	34 4	(0 16,	32 8–36 2)	24	34 6	(0 27,	33 5–35 0)	5
Needle color value	4 4	(0 09,	3 0–5 0)	27	4 4	(0 07,	3 6–5 1)	47	4 5	(0 09,	3 9–5 4)	22	4 8	(0 13,	37–61)	24	4 6	(0 19,	4 1–5 0)	5
Needle color chroma	4 6	(0 08,	3 5–5 0)	27	4 5	(0 06,	3 0–5 0)	47	4 2	(0 14,	2 5–5 0)	22	4 0	(0 16,	2 4–5 0)	24	4 8	(0 13,	4 3–5 0)	5
Needle length (cm)	19 8	(0 44,	14 4–24 3)	30	16 8	(0 29,	13 0–20 5)	48	112	(0 27,	9 2–14 4)	23	14 7	(0 45,	11 2–19 8)	24	15 6	(0 57,	14 8–17 9)	5
Needle length/fascicle length	8 1	(0 28,	5 8–12 8)	30	7 4	(0 15,	5 8–10 0)	48	6 1	(0 22,	4 2–7 8)	23	6 4	(0 26,	4 5–9 9)	23	9 3	(0 36,	8 2–10 4)	5
Needles per fascicle	3 0	(0 002,	2 99–3 04)	30	3 0	(0 002,	2 97–3 07)	48	2 6	(0 06,	2 2–3 0)	23	3 0	(0 03,	2 7–3 5)	24	2 4	(0 11,	2 2–2 8)	5
Needle thick (arbitrary units)	45 9	(0 49,	41 9–54 6)	30	47 8	(0 51,	37 6–58 8)	48	46 4	(0 68,	39 4–53 4)	23	44 8	(0 87,	34 4–51 1)	24	49 7	(0 61,	47 4–51 0)	5
Adaxial resin ducts/needle	0 8	(0 04,	0 25–1 22)	30	0 8	(0 04,	0 1–1 5)	48	0 9	(0 10,	0 3–2 5)	23	1 2	(0 09,	0 7–2 4)	24	1 5	(0 35,	0 6–2 6)	5
Abaxial resin ducts/needle	2 6	(0 15,	1 2–3 9)	30	2 3	(0 13,	0 1–4 1)	48	2 4	(0 15,	1 5–3 9)	23	2 4	(0 18,	0 8–4 4)	24	3 9	(0 60,	2 1–5 6)	5
Small resin ducts/needle	3 2	(0 19,	0 9–4 9)	30	2 8	(0 17,	0 4–5 2)	48	3 1	(0 25,	1 8–6 4)	23	3 4	(0 27,	1 1–6 4)	24	5 4	(0 98,	2 5–8 2)	5
Hypodermal cell layers	3 2	(0 04,	2 7–3 7)	30	3 4	(0 03,	2 7–3 9)	48	4 1	(0 05,	3 6–4 4)	23	4 1	(0 06,	3 4–4 5)	24	4 7	(0 06,	4 5–4 9)	5
Branches																				
Branches per whorl	4 4	(0 13,	2 7–6 0)	30	3 7	(0 11,	1 9–5 6)	50	3 0	(0 17,	2 0–4 6),	23	3 4	(0 25,	1 6–6 6)	23	2 3	(0 11,	1 1–1 6)	5
Branch angle (degrees from vert.)	56	(1 8,	30–75)	30	51	(17,	30–79)	50	50	(23,	31–76)	23	48	(31,	30–79)	24	36	(19,	31–40)	5
Seed cones																				
Cone length (mm)	101 4	(2 48,	63 6–121 7)	25	88 7	(1 24,	72 5–103 0)	36	70 7	(2 20,	52 4–92 6)	22	74 9	(2 51,	60 2–99 2)	20	711	(2 46,	64 8–77 1)	5
Cone width (mm)	77 1	(1 35,	56 3–88 6)	25	71 6	(0 73,	63 6–81 4)	36	61 5	(1 08,	53 1–69 1)	22	62 6	(1 77,	47 6–75 6)	20	63 3	(2 18,	58 6–68 9)	5
Cone form (width/length)	0 80	(0 03,	0 70–1 50)	25	0 84	(0 03,	0 80–1 80)	36	0 90	(0 02,	0 70–1 00),	22	0 86	(0 02,	0 80–1 00)	20	0 90	(0 03,	0 80–1 00)	5
Seeds																				
Seed length (mm)	7 5	(0 08,	6 9–8 1)	23	7 6	(0 16,	6 5–8 4)	14	6 3	(0 09,	5 4–6 9)	17	6 4	(0 18,	5 1–7 4)	16	7 0	(0 12,	6 5–7 2)	5
Seed width (mm)	4 9	(0 05,	4 3–5 3)	23	4 9	(0 08,	4 5–5 5)	14	4 1	(0 05,	3 6–4 6)	17	4 3	(0 09,	3 8–4 9)	16	4 5	(0 10,	4 2–4 7)	5
Seed + wing length (mm)	32 3	(0 58,	24 2–37 0)	23	24 8	(0 62,	20 2–29 5)	14	22 9	(0 63,	18 0–27 6)	17	23 3	(0 68,	18 2–26 2)	15	23 1	(0 78,	20 8–24 9)	5
Seed wing widest (base to tip)	0 36	(0 02,	0 30–0 50)	23	0 46	(0 01,	0 40–0 50)	14	0 44	(0 02,	0 30–0 50)	17	0 44	(0 01,	0 40–0 50)	15	0 48	(0 02,	0 40–0 50)	5
Seed form (length/width)	1 52	(0 01,	1 40–1 60)	23	1 57	(0 02,	1 40–1 70)	14	1 52	(0 01,	1 40–1 60)	17	1 48	(0 02,	1 30–1 60)	16	1 56	(0 02,	1 50–1 60)	5
Wing length, absolute (mm)	24 8	(0 57,	16 1–28 9)	23	16 6	(0 70,	13 0–21 8)	14	16 4	(0 67,	10 0–21 1)	17	15 5	(1 47,	15 1–19 3)	16	16 1	(0 68,	14 3–17 7)	5
Wing length, proportional	4 34	(0 08,	3 00–4 90)	23	3 26	(0 10,	2 90–4 10)	14	3 62	(0 09,	3 10–4 30)	17	3 59	(0 07,	3 30–4 00)	15	3 30	(0 06,	3 20–3 50)	5

110° and 112.5°. To the east, plots 114, 115, 116, and 117 were characterized by 2.35, 2.25, 2.44, and 2.52 needles per fascicle, respectively. Trees in plots 110, 111, and 113 and proximal plots west of 112.5° possessed fewer than 3.5 hypodermal cell layers in needle corners (C14). Eastward from 110° meridian, plots 114, 115, 116, and 117 had more than 4.0 hypodermal cell layers. These data confirmed earlier interpretations of this compact transition zone, using data collected both in situ and from provenance trials (Critchfield 1984, Korstian 1924, Read 1980, Weidman 1939, Wells 1964a).

Step 2: analyses of variance—

One-way analyses of variance of characteristics yielded highly significant plot differences for all characteristics except cone shape (C17) (table 2). Relatively low F-values were recorded for branch angle (C4), hue, value, and chroma of needle color (C5, C6, and C7), needle thickness (C11), needle resin ducts (C12, C13, and C22), and seed form (C23).

One possible explanation for relatively insignificant differences among plots for hue, value, and chroma of needle color may be the difficulty of subjectively evaluating these characteristics on samples received over a period of months and therefore varying in maturity and freshness. Relatively low F-values were calculated for some quantitative characteristics, i.e., branch angle (C4), needle thickness (C11), and needle resin ducts (C12, C13, and C22). Within-plot variance for these characteristics is relatively large on a range-wide basis.

Step 3: cluster analyses—

Cluster analyses using selected foliar characteristics did not yield clear racial boundaries. The first cluster delineated two general races separated at 112.5° meridian. Plots 110, 111, and 113 clustered with Rocky Mountains plots. Plots 96, 108, 109, 124, 125, 182, and 183 clustered with western plots. Many anomalies were present, particularly in the western grouping. Plots 38, 41, 52, 79, 97, 98, 105, 107, 123, 159, 158, 167, and 44 all clustered with eastern races while plots 23, 133, and 135 clustered with western races. Plot 44, as will be discussed later, showed evidences of natural hybridization with Jeffrey pine (*P. jeffreyi* Grev. & Balf. in A. Murray). This may explain why it grouped with eastern races.

Cluster analyses suggested presence of several transition zones. These zones separated five geographic races:

- Pacific: including California west of the summits of the Cascade Range and the Sierra Nevada and moist western valleys of Oregon and Washington
- North Plateau: including the Inland Empire and eastern slopes of both the Cascade Range and Sierra Nevada

- Rocky Mountains: including all areas east of the Continental Divide in Montana and Wyoming and central Rocky Mountains north of latitude 41°N except for the central high plains and the southwest described next
- Central High Plains: including drainages of the White, Niobrara, and Platte Rivers in South Dakota and Nebraska
- Southwest: including an area generally in Arizona and associated areas of New Mexico subject to bimodal rainfall patterns with monsoonal summer rains generated in the Gulf of California

Cluster analyses were useful for delineating five racial boundaries. They were too ambiguous to draw boundaries within the five racial boundaries comparable to those drawn by Read (1980, 1983).

Step 4: analysis of east-west races—
Stepwise discriminant analysis, using both forward and backward procedures, chose needle length (C8), needle thickness (C11), adaxial resin ducts (C12), and hypodermal cell layers (C14) as four discriminators between western and eastern races. However, a discriminant analysis using all foliar characteristics provided the best reclassification percentage (95 percent correct for eastern races and 100 percent correct for western races). The high percentage of correct classification confirms the long-recognized distinction between taxonomic varieties of *ponderosa* and *scopulorum*.

Only plots 110, 111, and 113 were misclassified as var. *ponderosa*. These plots are adjacent to the boundary between varieties in Montana. Cluster analysis had grouped these with other eastern plots. Contradictions between the two analyses and geographic locations indicate that these plots are part of a transition zone centered in Helena, Montana. This finding agrees with Read's (1980) narrow transition zone in Montana.

Step 5a: simultaneous analyses of hypothesized races—
Forward and backward stepwise discriminant procedures selected number of branches per whorl (C3), branch angle (C4), needle length (C8), needle length/ fascicle sheath length (C9), needles per fascicle (C10), needle thickness (C11), adaxial resin ducts (C12), and hypodermal cell layers (C14) as best discriminators among five races considered simultaneously. Canonical discriminant analysis, using these variables, indicated that five races are distinctly different (table 4 and fig. 2). Three evidences of this difference are:

- Very highly significant correlation coefficient (0.92, $p < 0.001$, table 4)
- Relatively large Eigen value (6.2, table 4)
- Large separation among group centroids (fig. 2).

Table 4—Results of a canonical discriminant analysis evaluating five ponderosa pine races simultaneously using only foliar characteristics

Branch or foliage character	Code	Standardized discriminant function coefficients	
		1	2
Branches per whorl	C3	0.2878	-0.1052
Branch angle	C4	0.2753	-0.1497
Needle length	C8	0.9154	1.2687
Needle fascicle ratio	C9	-0.1594	-0.1626
Needles per fascicle	C10	0.0763	0.8619
Needle thickness	C11	0.4107	-0.6150
Adaxial resin ducts	C12	-0.5238	0.1064
Hypodermal cell layers	C14	-1.6595	1.3356
Eigen value		6.24	0.91
P-value		0.0001	0.0001
Adj. canonical correction		0.923	0.647

Source: Diebel.

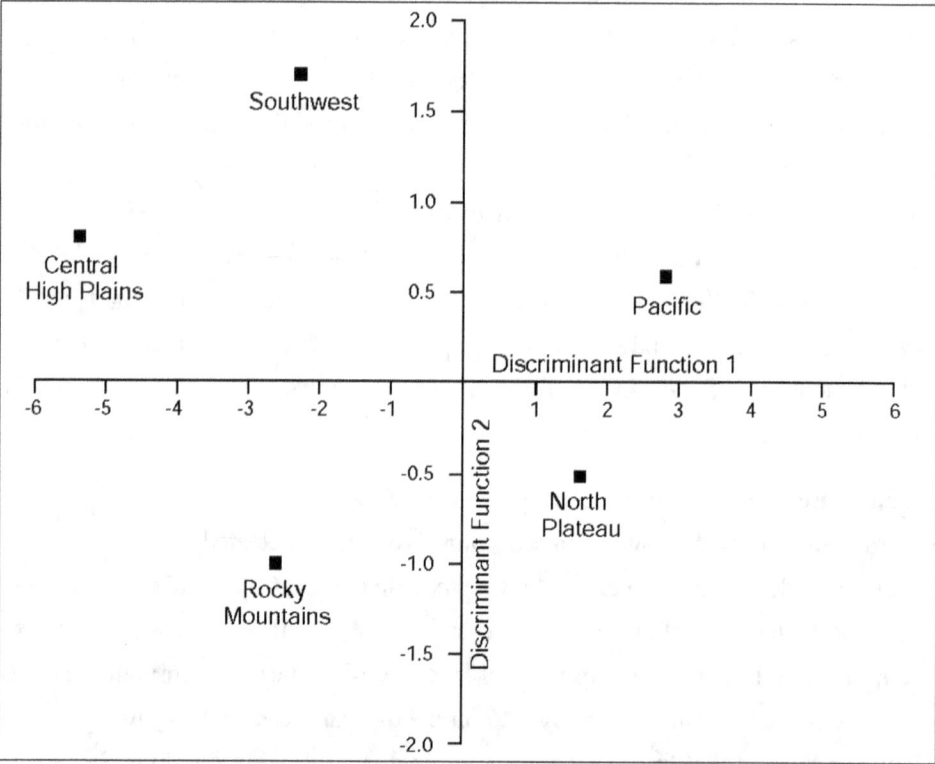

Figure 2—Scatter plot of group centroid values for each hypothesized race of ponderosa pine on the axes of the first two canonical discriminant functions (source: Kenneth Diebel).

Discriminant analysis correctly reclassified 94 percent of plots from the Rocky Mountains race. Only two plots (10 and 11) were misclassified. Plot 10 was classified as belonging to the North Plateau race, and plot 11 to the Southwestern race. Plot 11 is located near the hypothesized boundary between the Southwestern and Rocky Mountains races. Its misclassification may be an indication of an introgressive transition zone between these races. Classification of plot 10 into the North Plateau race is an anomaly. No climatic, elevational, or geographic affinity exists between plot 10 and the North Plateau race.

All plots from the Central High Plains race were correctly reclassified. This was also the case for both the Pacific and Southwestern races.

Ninety-four percent of plots from the North Plateau race were correctly reclassified. Plots 34, 53, and 119 were misclassified as belonging to the Pacific race. Plot 53 is located near the hypothesized boundary between these races. This misclassification may be related to a transition zone that will be discussed in the next section. There is no obvious explanation for misclassification of plots 34 and 119.

The high percentage of correctly reclassified plots is strong evidence of appropriateness of hypothesized racial designations. Potential transition zones among five geographically adjacent races were compared separately. Results of these paired comparisons are summarized in the following section.

Step 5b: analyses of adjacent races—
Characteristics selected for discriminating between geographically adjacent races allowed correct classification of 86 percent of plots for all comparisons. Needle length (C8) was the best overall discriminant foliar characteristic among races (table 2). Hue (C5), value (C6), and chroma (C7) of foliage color were characteristics providing poorest discrimination. Other foliar characteristics were of intermediate value; that is, they were useful in discriminating between some, but not all, races. No cone or seed variable was singularly best or poorest discriminator between adjacent races (table 3).

Paired comparisons of selected characteristics (using student's t-test) and a multivariate comparison based upon those selected traits (Hoetelling's t-test) (table 5) generally reinforced appropriateness of five racial boundaries.

Pacific vs. North Plateau—Foliar characteristics useful for discriminating between these two races were number of branches per whorl (C3), needle length (C8), and needle thickness (C11). Using these three characteristics, 89.5 percent of Pacific plots could be correctly classified, and 86.2 percent of North Plateau plots could be correctly classified.

Table 5—Results of multivariate (Hoetelling) comparisons between adjacent races and of univariate (student's t-test) comparisons between discriminating characteristics of adjacent races (by Diebel)

Multivariate Comparisons

Races compared	Branch and foliage	Seed cone and seed
	----------- $P > F$ -----------	
Pacific vs. North Plateau	0.001	N.A.*
North Plateau vs. Rocky Mountains	0.001	0.001
Rocky Mountains vs. Southwest	0.001	0.008
Rocky Mountains vs. Central High Plains	0.001	0.001
Southwest vs. Pacific	0.001	0.001

Univariate Comparisons

Branch/foliage	Means	Code	$P > F$	Cone or seed	Means	Code	$P > F$
Pacific vs. North Plateau							
Branches per whorl	4.4–3.7	C3	0.001	Seed wing length	4.3–3.3	C25	0.001
Needle length	198–168	C8	0.001	proportional (=C20 / C18)			
Needle thickness	45.9–47.8	C11	0.001				
North Plateau vs. Rocky Mountains							
Needle length	168–112	C8	0.001	Seed+wing length	24.8–22.9	C20	0.052
Hypodermal cell layers	3.4–4.1	C14	0.001	Cone form	0.84–0.90	C17	0.004
				Seed form	1.57–1.52	C23	0.312
				Seed wing length absolute (=C20–C18)	16.6–16.4	C24	0.753
Rocky Mountains vs. Southwest							
Needle length	112–147	C8	0.001	Seed form	1.52–1.48	C23	0.492
Needles per fascicle	2.6–3.0	C10	0.001	Seed wing length	16.4–15.5	C24	0.375
Needle thickness	46.4–44.8	C11	0.244	absolute (=C20–C18)			
Hypodermal cell layers	4.08–4.07	C14	0.352	Seed wing length	3.62–3.59	C25	0.433
				proportional (=C20 / C18)			
Rocky Mountains vs. Central High Plains							
Foliage length	21.1–42.2	C2	0.001	Seed+wing length	22.9–23.1	C20	0.935
Needle length	112–156	C8	0.001	Seed wing length	16.4–16.1	C24	0.500
Adaxial resin ducts	0.9–1.5	C12	0.011	absolute (=C20–C18)			
Hypodermal cell layers	4.1–4.7	C14	0.001				
Southwest vs. Pacific							
Years needles green	4.3–3.9	C1	0.194	Cone form	0.86–0.80	C17	0.001
Foliaged length	21.8–25.1	C2	0.483	Seed+wing length	23.3–32.3	C20	0.001
Branch angle	48–56	C4	0.023				
Needle length	147–198	C8	0.001				
Adaxial resin ducts	1.2–0.8	C12	0.001				
Hypodermal cell layers	4.1–3.2	C14	0.001				

*N.A. = not available.

Misclassified plots included plots 33, 34, 38, 107, and 119 in North Plateau and plots 44, 52, 80, and 81 in Pacific. Misclassified plots were examined and judged neither to be associated with any particular climatic or elevational pattern nor the border between these races. Plot 44, located at 6,000 ft elevation east of Placerville, California, in a known region of introgression between ponderosa pine and Jeffrey pine, seemed to be intermediate between these two species. Other misclassified Pacific plots were on the border delineating Pacific from North Plateau. This suggests either a gradual transition between these races along that boundary or a meandering boundary where a straight line has been proposed (fig. 1). Sturgeon's (1979) data supported location of this boundary and a major turning point at approximately 41°40'N, 122°10'W.

In a univariate test, three discriminant foliar characteristics differed significantly between Pacific and North Plateau plots (table 5). Pacific trees had longer, thinner needles (table 3). Pacific trees also had more branches per whorl. These features make crowns of Pacific trees particularly distinguishable. Long needles, generally a mesic characteristic, may be a result of higher available moisture in the maritime climate west of the crests of both the Sierra Nevada and Cascade Range.

Only one cone or seed character—proportional length of seed wing (C25)— was found to be useful in discriminating North Plateau race from the Pacific race. On the basis of this characteristic, 92 percent of North Plateau plots and 100 percent of the Pacific plots were correctly classified. Only plot 79, at the south end of Puget Sound, was misclassified, suggesting it should be included in the Pacific race.[4][5] Haller found:

> … North Plateau cones are usually heavier for their size and have more phyllotactic spirals than those from the Pacific race. They look denser. For me, this is the most easily observable difference between the two races. Cones from the North Plateau also are often smaller than those from the Pacific race, especially those from the western Sierra Nevada.

Statistics from this study confirm Haller's points, but Diebel did not find statistically significant differences.

Pacific race includes western mesic portions of Oregon and Washington. Haller's (1965) coastal ecotype, based on his in situ observations of adult trees, supports boundaries for the Pacific race. Haller and Vivrette (2011) named his coastal ecotype *Pinus ponderosa* var. *pacifica*.

---

[4] Haller, J.R. (retired professor, Univ. of California at Santa Barbara) 1992. Telephonic conversation with this author: "My numbers for the seed/wing proportion at this site support your conclusion."

[5] Haller, J.R. 1992. Personal letter to this author.

North Plateau vs. Rocky Mountains—Foliar morphological characteristics to discriminate between North Plateau and Rocky Mountains races were needle length (C8) and number of hypodermal cell layers in needle corners (C14). Just these two characteristics yielded 97.7 and 94.5 percent correct reclassification of North Plateau and Rocky Mountains plots, respectively.

Only plots 98, 110, and 111 were misclassified. Plots 110 and 111 are east of the Continental Divide at the border between the two races (fig. 1). These plots generally coincide with Read's (1980) narrow transition zone surrounding Helena, Montana. Plot 98 commonly was an anomaly in cluster analysis. Plot 98 is located approximately 27 mi south and 11 mi east of a known site of *P. washoensis* on Promontory Mountain, British Columbia (Critchfield 1984). Thus, trees from plot 98 may be introgressants or, more likely, Washoe pine.

On the basis of univariate analyses, North Plateau and Rocky Mountains races differed significantly in needle length (C8) and number of hypodermal cell layers in the corners of needles (C14) (table 5).

The Rocky Mountains race had the shortest needles of all races (5 in) and more hypodermal cell layers than the North Plateau race (table 2). Short needles and a thick hypodermis may enable ponderosa pine to survive harsher conditions during both summer and winter in truly continental climates.

Four cone and seed characteristics—cone form (C17), length of seed plus wing (C20), seed form (C23), and absolute length of seed wing (C24)—were useful discriminators between North Plateau and Rocky Mountains races (table 5). Using these four characteristics, 100 percent of the North Plateau plots and 95 percent of Rocky Mountains plots were correctly classified. Only plot 95 was misclassified in Rocky Mountains. Of four cone discriminators, only cone form (C17) was found to differ significantly at the 5 percent level between the Rocky Mountains and North Plateau races.

On the basis of multivariate comparisons of both cone and foliar characteristics, the North Plateau race differed very significantly (p < 0.001) from the Rocky Mountains race.

Rocky Mountains vs. Southwest—Rocky Mountains and Southwestern races were discriminated on the basis of needle length (C8), number of needles per fascicle (C10), needle thickness (C11), and number of hypodermal cell layers in needle corners (C14) (table 5). Classification of Rocky Mountains plots was 86.1 percent correct. Southwestern plots were 95.6 percent correctly reclassified; only plot 140, at high elevation near the northern boundary of the Southwestern race, was misclassified.

Rocky Mountains plots 1, 3, 7, 12, 166, and 175 were misclassified as Southwestern. All of these plots are located near the southern boundary of the Rocky Mountains race. This suggests presence of a relatively broad transition zone between the Rocky Mountains and Southwestern races, centered on "Four Corners" (the meeting point of Utah, Colorado, New Mexico, and Arizona). As Read (1980) illustrated, this boundary has been difficult to define. Very intensive sampling will be needed to define trends within the zone.

On the basis of univariate analyses, the Rocky Mountains and Southwestern races differed significantly in number of needles per fascicle (C10) and needle length (C8). Rocky Mountains trees had shorter needles and fewer needles per fascicle than Southwestern trees (table 2). Differences in needle thickness (C11) and number of hypodermal cell layers (C14) were not significant at the 5 percent level. Frequent and heavy summer rains and milder winters in the southwest probably have contributed to evolution of these racial differences.

On the basis of three selected seed discriminators—seed form (C23), absolute length of seed wing (C24), and proportional length of seed wing (C25)—91 percent of Rocky Mountains plots and 82 percent of Southwestern plots were correctly classified. In the Rocky Mountains, plots 175, 117, and 115 were misclassified, and in Southwestern, plots 129 and 190 were misclassified. The relatively high percentage of misclassified plots may be due to small differences between races for the selected discriminators.

The Rocky Mountains race differed statistically from the Southwestern race in multivariate comparisons using data on branches, foliage, cones, and seeds (table 5). However, in univariate comparisons no cone characteristic (C23, C24, or C25) differed significantly between the Rocky Mountains and Southwestern races (table 5).

Rocky Mountains vs. Central High Plains—The Rocky Mountains and Central High Plains races were 100 percent correctly reclassified by comparing foliage length (C2), needle length (C8), number of adaxial resin ducts (C12), and number of hypodermal cell layers (C14). The Rocky Mountains and Central High Plains races also differed significantly from one another in multivariate foliar comparisons (table 5).

All four traits used in a univariate test of differences between the Rocky Mountains and Central High Plains races differed significantly (table 5). Trees of the Central High Plains retained their needles 1 less year (4.7 vs. 5.7). Distance from branch tip to oldest green needles for the Central High Plains was twice that for the Rocky Mountains (1.3 vs. 0.7 ft). Needles from the Central High Plains were considerably longer than those from the Rocky Mountains (6.1 vs. 4.6 in). The Central High Plains also had more adaxial resin ducts (1.6 vs. 0.9) and more hypodermal cell layers (4.7 vs. 4.0) than did the Rocky Mountains.

Foliar characteristics of Central High Plains' trees appear to be contradictory with respect to drought hardiness. For example, more hypodermal layers may yield greater drought avoidance, whereas longer needles and much more foliage on the branch would appear to be counterproductive from the standpoint of water conservation. Trees of the Central High Plains have more resin ducts (both adaxial and abaxial) than all other races, which may impart a higher resistance to injury or damage from inclement weather, insects, and diseases.

Analyses of cone and seed characteristics between the Rocky Mountains and Central High Plains races were less definitive. Discriminant analysis based on length of seed plus wing (C20) and absolute length of seed wing (C24) yielded 85.7 percent correct classification of the Rocky Mountains plots (misclassified were plots 19, 114, and 117), and 80 percent correct classification of the Central High Plains plots (plot 26 was misclassified). Because misclassified plots show little geographic affinity, it would appear that these two taxa are not solidly differentiated on the basis of cone and seed characters. Although results of the univariate t-test showed non-significant differences, Hoetelling's multivariate t- test confirmed a statistically significant difference of the Rocky Mountains race from the Central High Plains race based on length of seed plus wing (C20) and absolute length of seed wing (C24) (table 5).

Southwestern vs. Pacific—Discriminant analysis of Southwestern and Pacific races yielded 100 percent correct classification of all plots based on number of years needles remain green (C1), foliage length (C2), branch angle (C4), needle length (C8), number of adaxial resin ducts (C12), and number of hypodermal cells (C14).

On the basis of univariate tests, the number of years needles remain green (C1) and foliage length (C2) did not differ significantly between these two races (table 5), but four other selected characteristics did differ significantly between the two races. Needles were one-third longer for Pacific than for Southwestern races (table 2). Adaxial resin ducts and hypodermal cell layers were more numerous in Southwestern than in Pacific races. These characteristics may help provide increased drought hardiness or pest resistance for the Southwestern race.

Discriminant analysis based on cone shape (C17) and length of seed plus wing (C20) also yielded 100 percent correct classification of Southwestern and Pacific races. Univariate analyses indicated significant differences between the Southwestern and Pacific races for both C17 and C20 (table 5).

On the basis of multivariate comparisons of foliar, cone, and seed data, the Southwestern race differed significantly from the Pacific race (table 5). These results support Critchfield's (1984) finding of no phylogenetic affinity between the Southwestern and Pacific races.

Step 6: provenance study of foliar discriminators—

Genetic control of foliar characteristics used in discriminant analyses was examined. Levels of significance were determined for effects on each characteristic of plantation, provenance, and plantation x provenance interaction (table 6). Of all characteristics used as discriminators of races, only branch angle (C4), used to discriminant the Pacific race from the Southwestern race, did not exhibit significant variation owing to provenance.

Relative contributions of plantation, seed source, and provenance x plantation interaction to total variance indicated that needle length (C8), needle thickness (C11), and number of hypodermal cell layers (C14) were under strongest genetic control (table 6). Needle length was picked as a discriminator of all races. Number of cell layers in corners was picked in four of five comparisons. Needle thickness was used in two of five comparisons.

Correlation between needle length of trees growing in plantations and in situ ($r = 0.64$), reported by Squillace and Silen (1962), supports this finding. Additionally, Grant et al. (1989) estimated a heritability value greater than 0.5 for length of primary needles on 3-year-old seedlings resulting from a nested mating design.

Wells (1964b) established that length of secondary needles, as measured in this study, was significantly correlated with four characteristics of climate at seed source. His data were from 2-year-old seedling progenies, grown in Michigan, from 33 eastern sources of variety *scopulorum*. He established coefficients of correlation (r) between needle length and four characteristics of climate:

Table 6—Partitioning of variance for each effect in the provenance experiment (by Diebel)

Branch or foliage character in plantations	Code		Percent of total variance due to:		
			Seed source (P)	Interaction (SS)	Error (P x SS)
Years needles remain green	C1	39.1**	4.5**	29.5**	26.9**
Branches per whorl	C3	43.7**	1.9**	4.2*	50.2*
Branch angle in tree top	C4	0.7**	1.5	2.9	87.9
Needle length	C8	68.8**	16.9**	5.1	9.2
Needle length/fascicle length	C9	30.2	9.7**	9.3**	50.8
Needles per fascicle	C10	0.3	4.0*	0.0	95.7
Needle thickness	C11	4.9**	12.2**	8.2*	74.7
Adaxial resin ducts in needles	C12	18.6**	2.0*	11.7*	67.7
Abaxial resin ducts in needles	C13	94.7**	1.4**	0.1	3.8
Hypodermal cell layers in needles	C14	7.0**	29.2**	7.3**	56.5

* Effect significant at p 0.05.

** Effect significant at p 0.01.

- Average spring temperature, r = 0.54
- Annual temperature range, r = -0.52
- Length of growing season, r = 0.38
- Day length at start of growing season, r = -0.51.

The above evidences demonstrate that characteristics measured in situ reflect, at least in part, real genetic differences among populations.

Step 7: correlations between characteristics, climate, and geography—
For the species as a whole, coefficients of correlation (r) between foliage, cone, and seed characteristics and climatic or geographic measures of site variability were usually significant (p < 0.05) or highly significant (p < 0.01). Within races, 182 correlations between characteristics of trees and either climatic or geographic variables were statistically significant (tables 7 and 8). To discuss each of these relationships is beyond the scope of this paper. Only some of the most interesting correlations for each race are considered.

Pacific Race

Only two foliar characteristics had multiple significant correlations with climatic variables. Years that needles remain green (C1) were significantly related to all but one climatic variable. Most of these correlations were negative indicating that years of needle retention increased as (1) precipitation decreased, (2) temperatures decreased, and (3) growing season became shorter. These relationships help to explain why years of needle retention (C1) increased significantly as elevation of plot increased. All of the foregoing would indicate that years of needle retention increase as conditions for growth become less favorable or more stressful.

Only one other foliar characteristic—needle length (C8)—had multiple significant correlations with climatic variables in the Pacific race. It was positively related to most of the climatic variables. Individual needles grew longer with increases in (1) summer precipitation, (2) growing season temperature, (3) growing season duration, and (4) seasonal temperature range. These relationships undoubtedly contributed to the negative correlation between needle length and elevation.

Surprising in the Pacific race was the significant, but contradictory, relationship of length of green foliage (C2) to two climatic variables: latitude and summer precipitation. Length of green foliage increased as latitude increased (northward through California and Oregon's coastal valleys to Puget Sound). However, as summer precipitation increased (toward the Pacific Northwest and upward into the mountains), length of green foliage decreased.

Effects of longitude and latitude varied greatly within this long, narrow race. Some of the geographic changes in characteristics were interesting. Branch angle

Table 7—Significant coefficients of correlation between characteristics of branches and foliage and characteristics of climate and plot locations (by Diebel)

Races and characteristics	Code	Precipitation July and August	Precipitation Annual	Jan. mean	Temperature Growing season	Temperature July mean	Range July–Jan.	Growing season length	Elevation	Location Longitude	Location Latitude
Pacific (27 or 30 plots)											
Years needles stay green	C 1	-0.52**	-0.48*	—	-0.70**	-0.47*	0.56**	-0.67**	0.65**	—	—
Foliage length	C 2	-0.43*	—	—	—	—	—	—	—	—	0.60**
Branch angle	C 4	—	—	—	—	—	—	—	—	0.35*	0.46*
Foliage color value	C 6	—	—	-0.43*	—	—	—	—	—	—	—
Foliage chroma	C 7	—	—	0.47*	—	—	—	—	—	—	—
Needle length	C 8	0.77**	—	—	0.64**	0.56*	-0.47*	0.78**	-0.59**	—	—
Needle length/sheath length	C 9	—	—	—	—	—	-0.60**	0.44*	-0.38*	—	—
Needle thickness	C11	—	—	0.62**	—	-0.53**	—	—	—	—	—
Adaxial resin ducts	C12	—	—	—	—	—	—	—	—	—	0.40*
Abaxial resin ducts	C13	—	—	—	—	—	—	—	—	—	0.38*
Hypodermal cell layers	C14	—	—	—	—	—	0.42*	—	0.54**	-0.59**	-0.57**
Total small resin ducts	C22	—	—	—	—	—	—	—	—	—	0.39*
North Plateau (47–50 plots)											
Years needles stay green	C 1	—	—	-0.29*	-0.41**	-0.33*	—	-0.51**	0.54**	—	-0.28*
Branch angle	C 4	0.41**	0.46**	—	—	—	—	—	0.29*	—	-0.39***
Foliage color value	C 6	—	—	—	—	—	—	-0.31*	—	—	—
Foliage chroma	C 7	—	—	—	0.35*	0.35*	—	—	—	—	—
Needle length	C 8	—	—	0.29*	0.49**	0.59***	—	0.51**	-0.33*	—	—
Needle fascicle ratio	C 9	—	—	0.32*	0.36*	0.55***	—	0.38**	—	—	—
Needles per fascicle	C10	—	—	—	—	-0.33*	—	—	—	—	—
Needle thickness	C11	—	—	—	—	—	—	—	—	0.29*	—
Rocky Mountains (22 or 23 plots)											
Foliage length	C 2	—	—	—	—	—	—	—	-0.33*	—	0.39*
Foliage hue	C 5	—	—	—	0.35*	0.35*	—	—	—	—	—
Foliage chroma	C 7	—	—	—	0.37*	—	—	—	-0.39*	—	0.39*
Needle length	C 8	—	—	—	—	0.43*	—	0.36*	-0.39*	—	—
Needle length/sheath length	C 9	—	—	—	0.41*	0.54***	—	0.34*	-0.56**	—	—
Needles per fascicle	C10	—	—	—	-0.39*	-0.48***	—	—	0.43**	0.63**	-0.48**

Table 7—Significant coefficients of correlation between characteristics of branches and foliage and characteristics of climate and plot locations (by Diebel) (continued)

| Races and characteristics | Code | Precipitation | | Temperature | | | | Growing season length | Elevation | Location | |
		July and August	Annual	Jan. mean	Growing season	July mean	Range July–Jan.			Longitude	Latitude
Needle thickness	C11	—	0.35*	—	—	0.41*	—	0.38*	—	—	—
Adaxial resin ducts	C12	—	0.41*	—	—	—	—	—	0.42*	0.37*	-0.39*
Hypodermal cell layers	C14	—	—	—	0.36*	0.37*	—	—	—	-0.59**	—
Total small resin ducts	C22	—	0.44*	—	—	—	—	—	—	—	—
Central High Plains (5 plots)											
Needles per fascicle	C10	—	—	—	—	—	—	—	—	-0.94*	—
Needle thickness	C11	-0.90*	—	—	—	0.88*	—	—	—	—	—
Adaxial resin ducts	C12	—	—	—	0.93*	—	—	—	—	-0.88*	—
Abaxial resin ducts	C13	—	—	—	—	—	—	0.97**	—	-0.90*	—
Total small resin ducts	C22	—	—	—	0.96**	—	—	—	—	-0.91*	—
Southwest (23 or 24 plots)											
Years needles stay green	C 1	—	-0.52*	—	—	—	-0.60**	—	—	—	0.53**
Foliage length	C 2	—	—	—	—	—	—	—	—	0.44*	0.45*
Branches per whorl	C 3	—	—	—	—	—	—	—	-0.50*	0.44*	—
Foliage hue	C 5	—	—	—	—	—	—	—	—	0.42*	—
Foliage color value	C 6	—	—	—	—	—	—	—	—	—	0.45*
Needle length	C 8	—	—	—	—	—	—	—	-0.43*	—	—
Needle length/sheath length	C 9	—	—	—	0.52*	0.49*	—	—	-0.71**	—	—
Needles per fascicle	C10	—	—	—	—	—	-0.57**	—	—	—	-0.52*
Needle thickness	C11	—	—	—	—	—	—	—	—	—	0.47*
Abaxial resin ducts	C13	—	—	-0.42*	—	—	0.58**	—	—	0.45*	0.57**
Total small resin ducts	C22	—	—	—	—	—	0.56**	—	—	0.46*	0.52*

* Coefficient significant at p < 0.05.

** Coefficient significant at p < 0.01.

Table 8—Significant coefficients of correlation between characteristics of cones and seeds and characteristics of both climate and plot locations (by Diebel)

Races and characteristics	Code	Precipitation July and August	Precipitation Annual	Temperature Jan mean	Temperature Growing season	Temperature July mean	Temperature Range July–Jan.	Growing season length	Elevation	Location Longitude	Location Latitude
Pacific (23 or 25 plots)											
Cone length	C15	0.57**	—	—	—	0.58**	—	—	—	—	—
Cone width	C16	0.50*	—	—	—	0.58**	—	—	—	—	—
Cone form	C17	-0.49*	—	—	—	-0.46*	—	—	—	—	—
Seed length	C18	—	—	—	—	—	—	—	—	-0.50*	—
Seed width	C19	—	—	—	—	—	—	—	—	-0.44*	—
Seed+wing length	C20	0.58**	—	0.47*	0.53*	0.69**	—	—	—	—	—
Seed wing widest	C21	—	—	—	—	—	-0.54*	—	—	—	—
Wing length, absolute	C24	0.62**	—	-0.51*	0.54*	0.74**	—	—	—	—	—
Wing length, proportional	C25	0.65**	—	—	0.49*	0.77*	—	—	—	—	—
North Plateau (14 or 36 plots)											
Cone width	C16	—	—	—	—	—	—	—	—	—	-0.34*
Wing length, proportional	C25	—	-0.65*	—	—	—	-0.59*	—	—	—	—
Rocky Mountains (17 or 22 plots)											
Cone length	C15	—	—	—	—	—	0.37*	—	—	0.66**	—
Cone width	C16	—	—	—	—	—	0.33*	—	—	0.42*	—
Seed length	C18	—	—	—	—	—	—	—	-0.45*	—	0.45*
Seed width	C19	—	—	—	—	0.47*	—	—	-0.55*	—	0.52*
Seed+wing length	C20	0.61**	0.49*	—	—	—	—	—	—	0.65**	—
Seed wing widest	C21	—	—	—	—	—	—	—	-0.68**	-0.59***	0.66**
Wing length, absolute	C24	0.61**	0.57**	—	—	—	—	—	—	0.67***	—
Wing length, proportional	C25	0.57**	0.52*	—	—	—	—	—	—	0.61**	—
Central High Plains (5 plots)											
Cone form	C17	—	—	—	-0.90*	-0.90*	—	0.89*	—	—	—
Seed form	C23	—	—	—	—	—	—	—	—	—	0.99**
Southwest (16 or 20 plots)											
Cone length	C15	0.57*	0.55*	—	—	—	—	—	—	0.57*	—
Cone width	C16	—	0.61**	—	—	0.46*	—	—	—	0.50*	—
Seed length	C18	—	—	0.73**	0.57*	—	—	0.74**	-0.56*	—	—
Seed width	C19	—	—	0.76**	—	—	0.66**	0.72**	—	—	—
Seed wing length	C20	—	—	—	—	—	—	—	-0.56*	—	—
Seed form	C23	—	—	—	0.55*	—	—	—	-0.55*	—	-0.59*
Wing length, proportional	C25	0.64*	—	—	—	—	—	—	—	0.66**	—

* Coefficient significant at p < 0.05.

** Coefficient significant at p < 0.01.

(C4) increased in northern and western plots. Hypodermal cell layers (C14) were more numerous at higher elevations; this also was the situation in the Rocky Mountains race. This significant relationship between number of hypodermal cell layers and elevation probably contributed to a negative relationship between number of hypodermal cell layers and longitude. In this race, the most eastern plots usually occurred at highest elevations. Both seed length (C18) and seed width (C19) decreased in the southern plots.

Haller (1962, p. 131) wrote: "Altitude also affects needle thickness. The needles of both *P. ponderosa* and *P. jeffreyi* are relatively thick at high elevations, and relatively thin at low elevations." However, in contradiction he later wrote:

> I found no increase at all in needle thickness with elevation in either of two elevational transects in the Sierra Nevada. In the San Bernardino Mountains, the only significant difference was between the lower elevation and mid elevation samples. This is probably anomalous, and may be related to the location of some of the low elevation trees in a moist, shady ravine.[6]

There was no significant correlation between needle thickness and elevation for this or any other race.

Haller (1962) reported for this race that proportional length of seeds to seed wings changed with elevation, but on subjecting his data to statistical analysis[7] he found differences were not significant. The only significant difference was between his low-elevation and mid-elevation sites in the San Bernardino Mountains. Longer wings at his mid-elevation site appeared to be related to larger cones there. However, correlations between proportional seed wing length (C25) and elevation were not significant for this or any other race.

Several interrelated cone and seed characteristics showed greater values with increased precipitation during July and August and with higher temperature during July. These characteristics were cone length (C15), cone width (C16), length of seed plus wing (C20), absolute wing length (C24), and proportional wing length (C25). Both growing season precipitation and July temperature (but not growing season temperature) positively contributed to bigger cones and seeds and to longer seed wings. These highly significant relationships did not exist for any other race. Only in the Rocky Mountains race did length of seed plus wing (C20), absolute wing length (C24), and proportional wing length (C25) show similar highly significant correlations with summer precipitation (and annual precipitation), but these characteristics were not correlated with climatic temperatures.

---

[6] Personal communication from J.R. Haller, March 1992.

[7] Personal communication from J.R. Haller, March 1992.

Ponderosa pine grows intermixed with Jeffrey pine at the upper limits of its elevational distribution from the southern Sierra Nevada north into the Cascade Range. In southern California areas of overlap, and possibly opportunities for hybridization, are somewhat greater.[8] That natural hybridization occurs between these species has been known for many years[9] (Haller 1962). Some ponderosa pines growing at highest elevations—both east of Placerville, California (plot 44), at 6,000 ft elevation on U.S. Highway 50, and west of La Moine (plot 64), near Mount Shasta in northern California—exhibited unusually long cones and other features that would indicate presence of natural hybrids with the longer-coned Jeffrey pine.

North Plateau race—Two foliar characteristics of the North Plateau race, like the Pacific race, had multiple significant correlations with climatic variables. Apparently for ponderosa pine's two western races, years of needle retention (C1) and length of needles (C8) differ strongly in association with climatic factors favoring growth. The negative correlation between needles per fascicle (C10) and July temperature would indicate a propensity for two-needled trees where summer temperatures are hotter. This same negative correlation was found for the Rocky Mountains race.

Within the North Plateau race, branch angle (C4) increased as:

- Annual precipitation increased
- Summer precipitation increased
- Elevation increased
- Latitude decreased

Branches of northern trees angled upward toward vertical, presumably as severity of winter and winter's snow loading would increase. Interestingly, branch angle was not significantly correlated with the severity of winter (January) temperatures.

One can only guess at biological significance of correlations between proportional length of seed wing (C25) and climatic variables. Wings that are longer in relation to seed length should fall more slowly, for extra wing length should not add significantly to weight of seed plus wing. Why relatively longer seed wings were found on plots having greater annual precipitation and greater range in mean temperature (July minus January means) is puzzling.

---

[8] Personal communication from J.R. Haller, March 1992.

[9] Unpublished data on file at USDA Forest Service's Institute of Forest Genetics, Placerville, CA.

Rocky Mountains race—No correlation between needle retention (C1) and either climatic or geographic variables was significant for this race. This contrasts sharply with situations for Pacific and North Plateau races and less sharply for the Southwestern race.

Needle length (C8) increased as the mean temperature in July increased and as the growing season became longer. In this race, as for races to the south and west, needles became shorter (C8) as elevation increased.

The number of needles per fascicle (C10) increased as the temperature during the growing season decreased and as July mean temperature decreased. Needles per fascicle increased at higher elevations as Haller (1965) had found, but this was true only for this race. Needles per fascicle increased in frequency toward the west and south within this race.

The number of adaxial resin ducts in needles (C12) increased toward the west, south, and higher elevations. As in the Central High Plains race, number of adaxial resin ducts was higher where climate was wetter.

Hypodermal cell layers (C14) were more numerous eastward and where temperatures were warmer during the growing season.

Both cone length and width (C15 and C16) increased westward. Seed length and width (C18 and C19) both decreased at higher elevations and northward. Length of seed plus wing (C20), absolute length of seed wing (C24), and proportional length of seed wing (C25) all increased westward. Longer seed wings also were found where precipitation was more abundant.

Central High Plains race—Although only five plots from this race were studied, analyses showed eight significant correlations between characteristics of foliage and climatic and geographic variables. Needle thickness (C11) increased significantly as precipitation during July and August growing season decreased. As July mean temperature increased, so did width of needles.

Number of needles per fascicle (C10) and numbers of both adaxial and abaxial resin ducts (C12 and C13) decreased westward. The finding about the number of adaxial resin ducts is of special interest, for it is opposite to the relationship for the Rocky Mountains race where adaxial resin ducts (C12) were significantly fewer but also decreased toward the east. Number of adaxial resin ducts also increased as growing season temperature increased, but the number of abaxial resin ducts increased as growing season lengthened.

Cone form was positively related to length of growing season but negatively related to both July mean temperature and temperature during the growing season. That is, cones were less elongate and more ovoid where growing season was longer and temperatures were cooler. Such high correlations for this characteristic were not found in any other race.

The highest correlation in this study (r = 0.99) was between seed form and latitude in the Central High Plains race. Range in latitude for five plots in this race was less than two degrees. Yet from south to north, a distance of about 93 mi, seeds became steadily and consistently longer in relation to width.

Southwestern race—The Southwestern race displayed patterns of internal variation similar to those of other races as well as some unique patterns. Years that needles remain green (C1) increased toward north and as annual precipitation decreased. Green foliage length (C2) increased toward both north and west. Number of branches per whorl (C3) decreased at higher elevations and eastward. Needles per fascicle (C10) decreased significantly northward, which one might expect considering that north is predominantly toward the two-needled Rocky Mountains race. Number of abaxial resin ducts (C13) increased toward both west and north, as was the case for the Rocky Mountains race.

Both length and width of cones (C15 and C16) increased westward parallel to the situation in the Rocky Mountains race. Proportional length of seed wing (C25) increased westward, as it did in the Rocky Mountains race. Both seed form (C23) and seed length (C18) decreased as elevation rose, but seed width did not change significantly with elevation. As a result, seeds were less elongate at higher elevations. Length of seed plus wing (C20) also decreased as elevation increased. Width of seed (C19) decreased northward, whereas the opposite was true for the Rocky Mountains race (located to the north and having narrowest seeds of all races). The narrowest seeds for ponderosa pine must be found somewhere in the transition zone between the Southwestern and Rocky Mountains races.

Smith (1977) characterized monoterpenes of southwestern ponderosa pine as having "large amounts of alpha-pinene and (delta-3-carene) and small amounts of beta-pinene, myrcene and limonene." The southern part of this race, Smith's Coronado Region and Chiricahua Zone, have "about 90 percent alpha-pinene with small or trace amounts of the other four major components."

Discussion

Racial differences and transition zones delineated here help clarify the taxonomy of ponderosa pines north of Mexico (fig. 3). Major morphological differences among races documented here were sufficient to cause early taxonomists to apply a unique epithet to each race except Central High Plains ponderosa pine.

Using seed collected for this study, Wells' provenance study (1964a, 1964b) confirmed four of the five races identified here. Significant genetic barriers to

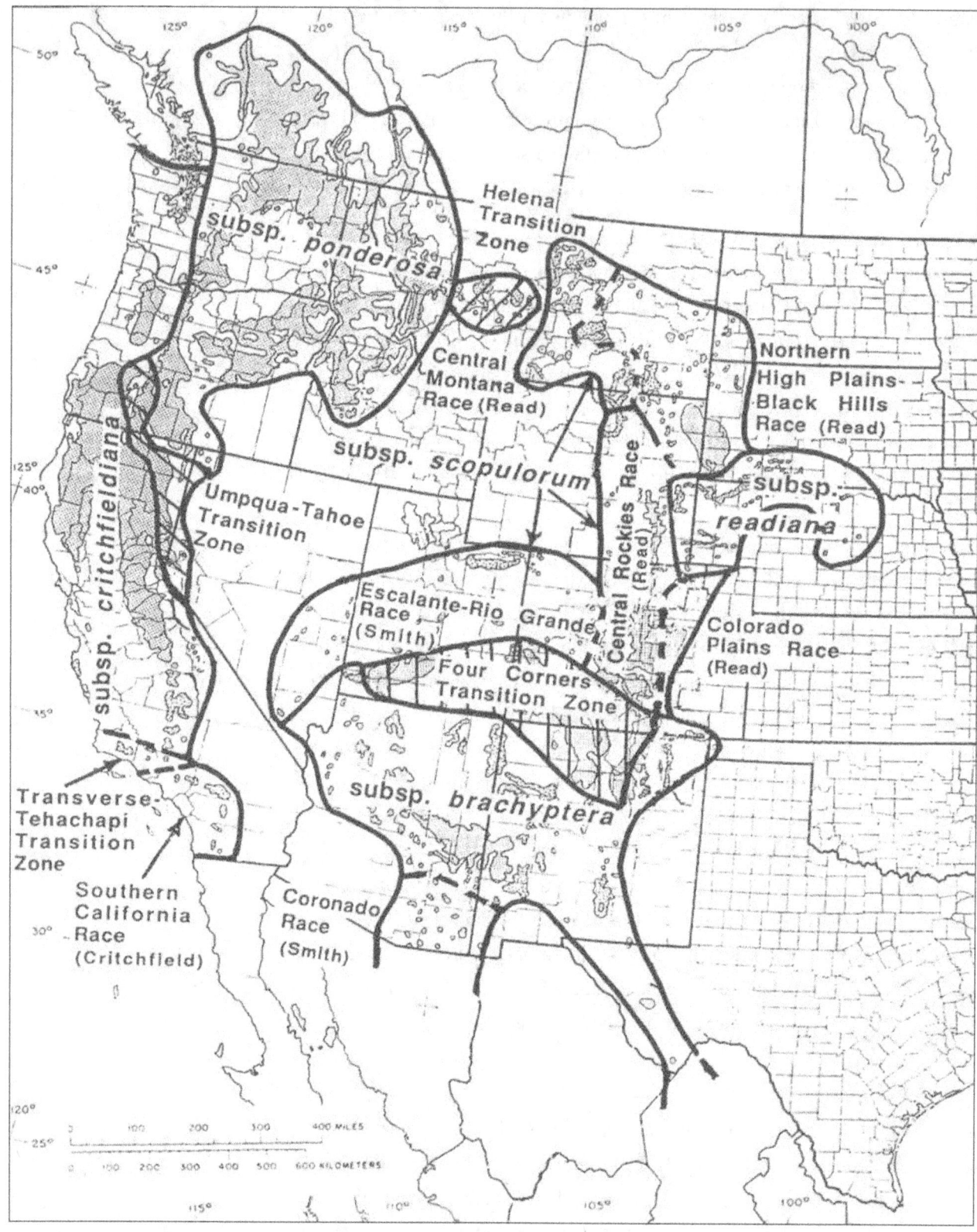

Figure 3—Distribution of ponderosa pine and boundaries of its taxonomic entities.

crossing among three races are evident or likely (Conkle and Critchfield 1988, Critchfield 1984,). Smith (1977) has established strong genetic differences among four of the five races in proportions of five monoterpenes in xylem oleoresin. Niebling and Conkle (1990) have established differences in allozymes between three of the five races.

In light of these collected evidences, ponderosa pine includes five subspecies and at least three, perhaps five, transition zones (Callaham 2013). These subspecies closely coincide with:

- Geographic races proposed by Weidman (1939)
- Ecotypes proposed by Wells (1964a) and Haller (1965)
- Regions and zones proposed by Smith (1977)
- Geographic clusters proposed by Read (1980, 1983).

Numerous, significant differences among subspecies are contrasted in the following sections.

Pacific vs. Columbia Ponderosa Pine

The Pacific race, designated here as Pacific ponderosa pine, differs significantly from the North Plateau race, designated here as Columbia ponderosa pine. Data shown here (tables 2, 3, and 5) and findings by others establish that these are two different taxa.

Critchfield (1984) reported from preliminary data that these taxa are partially isolated by reproductive barriers that reduce crossability to 50 percent; however, he went on to write: "Although these data indicate the probable existence of a genetic barrier, they are too limited for a reliable estimate of its magnitude."

Smith (1977) found significant differences between these taxa in xylem turpentine chemistry. Monoterpenes of Pacific ponderosa pine are characterized by high amounts of both beta-pinene (27 to 45 percent) and delta-3-carene (35 to 41 percent, plus considerable myrcene (20 to 21 percent) and limonene (18 to 22 percent), whereas monoterpenes of Columbia ponderosa pines are characterized by very high delta-3-carene (48 to 53 percent), less myrcene (19 to 21 percent), and little to very little limonene (7 to 12 percent). Both taxa produce very little alpha-pinene (12 to 19 percent). Smith proposed (1977) and confirmed by later research[10] that amount of each of the five primary monoterpenes is controlled by a single gene with two additive alleles at the locus. Smith also noted that color of resin exuding from Pacific ponderosa pine "tends toward yellow and dark amber," but he did not comment on color of resin from Columbia ponderosa pine.

---

[10] Personal communication from Richard H. Smith (retired entomologist).

Smith (1981) made cogent observations of differences in the color of immature cones. Those of Pacific ponderosa pine were green to yellow-green. Those of Columbia ponderosa pine were red to purple on the majority of trees; less than 50 percent of the trees had green to yellow-green cones. Mixtures of immature cone colors occurred in northeastern California and south-central Oregon, where Smith identified the transition zone between Pacific and Columbia ponderosa pines. He also observed for Columbia ponderosa pine "that higher elevation stands generally will have higher frequencies of darker (red to purple immature) cones."

Niebling and Conkle (1990) estimated, on the basis of differences in allozymes, that average genetic distance between these two taxa was small; however, they recognized that trees they sampled, and called Pacific race, actually were growing in the transition zone between Pacific and Columbia ponderosa pines. Therefore, their published estimate of genetic distance between these two taxa probably is conservative.

Two plots in southern California did not differ significantly from the rest of Pacific ponderosa pine. Haller (1962), after studying morphology of ponderosa pines growing at several locations in southern California, concluded: "They are about as variable as in the western Sierra Nevada ... (and most characters) are within the usual ponderosa range on nearly all individuals ... (except that) the cones are notably smaller and denser ... ."

There is no basis for dividing Pacific ponderosa pine into northern and southern forms as was proposed initially by Weidman (1939). Wells (1964b) proposed that his North Plateau ecotype included the Willamette Valley, but he concluded: "The two Willamette Valley sources (actually my two sources) were different from the (North Plateau) sources in several characters ... ." He then included my two plots from the Willamette Valley of Oregon with all other Pacific sources. Haller's (1965) coastal ecotype, based on observations of trees growing in situ, is synonymous with Pacific ponderosa pine.

An isolated but significant stand of ponderosa pine at southeastern corner of Puget Sound (Fort McClellan, Washington, see plot 79, fig. 1) at first analysis was considered to be associated with the North Plateau race. Subsequent analyses showed it belongs with Pacific ponderosa pine and may be the northernmost stand of that taxon. Haller[11] supports its being Pacific ponderosa pine but knew of a population growing still farther north in the Skagit River Valley in British Columbia, just north of the international boundary. He wrote: " ... at 1,700 ft elevation, that appears to be closer to Pacific ponderosa pine than to Columbia ponderosa pine."

---

[11] Personal communication from J.R. Haller, March 1992.

These taxa are separated sharply by the crest of the Cascade Range in Oregon and Washington. A very short, narrow Columbia Gorge transition zone, near Hood River, Oregon, must occur but was not studied. Discontinuous populations growing along the Columbia River provide stepping-stones for gene transfer through the Cascade Range. Sorenson (1994), studying growth responses in a provenance study, found that nine populations from this transition zone differed significantly from immediately adjacent Columbia ponderosa pines.

The combined barriers of the crest of the Sierra Nevada and the Mojave and Sonoran Deserts in southern California and Arizona cleanly separate Pacific ponderosa pine from ponderosa pine growing in the Great Basin and in the Southwest.

Smith (1977) presented evidence—less delta-3-carene and more beta-pinene—for a southern California race (his San Jacinto Region) south of a narrow transition zone in the Transverse Range and Tehachapi Mountains. Critchfield (1984) and Conkle and Critchfield (1988), without further data or analysis, mapped Smith's region and transition zone. Detailed study is needed of the characteristics of foliage, cones, and resins from trees growing in this transition zone and in southern California.

Transverse/Tehachapi transition zone—

The Transverse Range system crosses California south of the Central Valley. Included is the Tehachapi Mountain Range extending easterly and southward separating the San Joaquin Valley to the northwest and the Mojave Desert to the southeast. This zone is designated here only because of Smith's (1977) findings of significant differences in oleoresin monoterpenes north and south of this zone. Neither this author nor Haller found differences between ponderosa pines growing north and south of this zone.

Umpqua-Tahoe transition zone—

Further intensive study will be necessary to delineate the long, sinuous, but relatively narrow, Umpqua-Tahoe transition zone. It separates these taxa in southern Oregon, northern California, and the eastern side of California in the rain shadow of the Sierra Nevada. Data presented here plus maps provided by Sturgeon (1979) and Smith (1981) show the zone meandering southerly through Oregon.

North of Mount Shasta, in far northern California, it turns east-southeasterly to Adin.[12] East of the summit of the Sierra Nevada it turns southerly and terminates near Lake Tahoe.

---

[12] Smith in a personal communication: The line passes through this area on the border between Modoc and Lassen Counties. Trees on these plots located only 10 mi to the north and east of Adin differed significantly from Pacific ponderosa pine.

This transition zone has not been extended to include six isolated stands growing in the rain shadow of southern Sierra Nevada near Bishop, California. Smith (1977) extended the transition zone to include these stands because he found monoterpenes from xylem oleoresin of these pines had relatively more (46 vs. 41 percent) delta-3-carene as was the case for pines growing farther north in the transition zone. Haller (1962) studied trees in one of Smith's stands and observed: "They grow only along the courses of perennial streams ... ." He described their morphology as "nearly typical and similar to that from his Ebbetts Pass transect (west of that pass on the Pacific slope of the Sierra Nevada), except for its highly variable bark." Conkle[13] found the size, shape, and color of ripening cones on trees growing on Haller's transect along Rock Creek in Inyo County and in five nearby stands to be indistinguishable from these characteristics of cones found on the western slopes of the Sierra Nevada.

Helena Transition Zone—

A relatively narrow transition zone, between meridians 110° and 112.5° near Helena in central Montana, separates Columbia ponderosa pine from Rocky Mountains ponderosa pine. The existence and location of this transition zone was first suggested by Weidman (1939), later supported by Wells (1964a) and Haller (1965), and confirmed with detailed data by Read (1980).

Rehfeldt,[14] from observations of seedlings grown in common gardens, writes: "All of western Montana is a transition zone. Exactly how far it extends into central and eastern Montana will have to await the results of our new studies, but my guess is that the transition extends all the way to the Black Hills." Rehfeldt's contention that genetic variation across Montana is continuous and distinctive is accepted, but his genetic variation was not expressed as significant morphological differences among trees growing in situ.

Smith (1977) also identified this Helena transition zone from a minor, but significant shift in monoterpenes occurring in xylem oleoresin. He placed the shift "at the Missouri River." It seems to relate to the barrier created by the Big Belt Mountains, the first significant range on the eastern flank of the northern Rocky Mountains. His plots 58 and 59—located only a few miles west of the longitude of Helena—differed from his plot 60—located just east of the Big Belt Mountains, about 40 mi east-northeast of Helena. Turpentine of plots to the west had significantly less of both alpha-pinene and beta-pinene and significantly more of delta-3 carene.

---

[13] Personal communication from M.T. Conkle, January 1992.

[14] Personal communication from Gerald E. Rehfeldt, January 27, 1992.

Rocky Mountains Ponderosa Pine

Both names, *Pinus ponderosa* var. *scopulorum* Engelm. and *P. ponderosa* subsp. *scopulorum* (Engelm.) E. Murray (1982), should be applied to Rocky Mountains ponderosa pine (Callaham 2013). The taxon others have called the Rocky Mountain ponderosa pine includes the Rocky Mountains, Central High Plains, and Southwestern races as they are described here. Findings about these subspecies lead to a smaller range for subsp. *scopulorum*. It encompasses (fig. 3):

- Northern interior and central interior ecotypes proposed by Wells (1964a)
- The "race found east of North Plateau" by Weidman (1939)
- Three or five of Read's (1980, 1983) delineated clusters

Morphological data disclosed here were much too variable to warrant further subdividing the Rocky Mountains ponderosa pine. Well's (1964a) nursery provenance study, from seed collected for the study reported here, supported existence of two to four ecotypes. Read (1980, 1983), using his growth performance data and Wells' maps, suggested existence of several races (fig. 3).

Rehfeldt (1990) mapped patterns of clinal genetic variation within Utah and western Colorado. Within the Rocky Mountains race of ponderosa pine, he separated Uinta Mountains (my plots 174 and 179 = Wells' 2258 and 2274) from Wasatch Plateau (my plots 164 and 165 = Wells' 1211 and 2116) and each of these from three overlapping populations on Fishlake Plateau, Tushar Mountains (my plot 180 = Wells' 2284), and Pine Valley Mountains (my plot 175 = Wells' 2274).

Smith (1977), studying five monoterpenes in xylem oleoresin, found no compelling evidence for subdividing Rocky Mountains ponderosa pine or for distinguishing it from either Columbia or Central High Plains ponderosa pines. However, monoterpenes of Rocky Mountains ponderosa pine differed significantly from those of both Pacific and Southwestern ponderosa pines.

Read,[15] after plotting Smith's data, concluded there were slight but recognizable differences in the amount of beta-pinene in monoterpenes between the Rocky Mountains (as mapped here) (21 to 28 percent) and Columbia ponderosa pine races (14 to 22 percent). After plotting Smith's data, I drew four similar conclusions:

- Northern Rocky Mountains ponderosa pine growing in central Montana, Wyoming, and South Dakota (Smith's plots 21 to 23, 60, and 61) differed significantly from Columbia ponderosa pine to the west [more alpha-pinene, (12) 14 to 16 percent vs. 12 to 13 percent, more beta-pinene, 23 to 32 percent vs. 14 to 25 percent, less delta-3-carene, 45 to 48 (53) percent vs. 50 to 53 percent, and less myrcene, 17 to 19 percent vs. 18 to 21 percent].

---

[15] Personal communication to W.B. Critchfield, September 1982.

- Western Rocky Mountains ponderosa pine growing in Utah and Nevada (Smith's plots 1, 42, 47, 62, 64, and 66) differed significantly from Columbia ponderosa pine growing to the north [more alpha-pinene, 17 to 26 percent vs. 12 to 13 percent, less delta-3-carene, 34 to 37 percent in Nevada, 44 to 49 (53) percent in Utah, vs. 51 to 53 percent, and less myrcene, 14 to 17 percent vs. 18 to 21 percent].
- Southeastern Rocky Mountains ponderosa pine growing in Colorado (Smith's plots 20, 48 to 49, 60) differed significantly from northern Rocky Mountains ponderosa pine [less beta-pinene, 19 to 20 percent vs. 27 to 28 percent, more delta-3-carene, 48 to 55 percent vs. 44 to 47 (52) percent, and less myrcene, 12 to 15 percent vs. 17 to 18 percent].
- Western Rocky Mountains ponderosa pine growing in Utah and Nevada (plots above) differed significantly from southeastern Rocky Mountains ponderosa pine growing in Colorado (plots above) [less delta-3-carene, 34 to 37 percent in Nevada, 44 to 49 (53) percent in Utah, vs. 48 to 55 percent, and more myrcene, 14 to 17 percent vs. 12 to 15 percent, and more limonene, 12 to 16 percent vs. 8 to 10 percent].

Rocky Mountains ponderosa pine differed from Pacific ponderosa pine by having less beta-pinene (21 to 28 percent vs. 27 to 45 percent), more delta-3-carene (37 to 55 vs. 35 to 41 percent), less myrcene (12 to 18 vs. 20 to 21 percent), and less limonene (8 to 19 vs. 18 to 22 percent). It differed from Southwestern ponderosa pine by having less alpha-pinene (12 to 29 vs. 38 to 74 percent), more beta-pinene, more delta-3-carene (37 to 55 vs. 15 to 42 percent), and more myrcene (12 to 18 vs. 5 to 15 percent).

Critchfield (1984) presented evidence that Rocky Mountains ponderosa pine is reproductively isolated from Pacific ponderosa pine. He estimated crossability of these taxa to be only 35 percent.

Niebling and Conkle (1990) determined genetic distances based on differences in allozymes. They concluded: Rocky Mountains ponderosa pine was separated by major genetic distances from both Pacific ponderosa pine (actually trees growing in the Umpqua-Tahoe transition zone as noted earlier) and Columbia ponderosa pine.

Lacking information about ponderosa pine growing in the mountains of southern Nevada west of Las Vegas, I accepted Smith's (1977) conclusion. He found that this population was related to typical Rocky Mountains ponderosa pine found to the north on scattered mountain in the Great Basin. Frank Hawksworth,[16] an authority on mistletoes, found the mistletoe infecting stands on Spring Creek Mountain, northwest of Las Vegas, Nevada, is the species infecting Pacific ponderosa pine

---

[16] Personal communication from Frank Hawksworth, March 1992.

rather than the species infecting Rocky Mountains ponderosa pine. Despite this anomalous host-parasite relation, I continue to believe that Rocky Mountains ponderosa pine found elsewhere in the Great Basin reaches its southern limit in southern Nevada. Haller[17] added "My data on needle length and needles per fascicle (Haller 1965), as well as other morphological characters, support your conclusion. The Rocky Mountains variety of white fir [*Abies concolor* (Gord. & Glend.) Lindl. ex Hildebr. var. *concolor*] also occurs in southern Nevada."

Central High Plains Ponderosa Pine

The Central High Plains ponderosa pine race differed significantly from Rocky Mountains ponderosa pine and is recognized as a separate taxon. The common name recognizes that stands of Rocky Mountains ponderosa pine occur on the high plains both north and south of this taxon.

Distribution of Central High Plains ponderosa pine cannot be mapped accurately. My five plots from this subspecies define an area south and east of the Black Hills and east of the Front Range in Wyoming but not extending southward into Colorado. My area for this taxon extends substantially farther to the west and south in Nebraska than the "east-low elevation" and "north-central Nebraska" clusters found by Read (1980, 1983). According to Read:[18] "The distribution should include White River that begins in northwest Nebraska and flows into South Dakota." Wells (1964a) mapped this taxon as being indistinguishable from subspecies *scopulorum* in the Black Hills and Montana, but distinct from that subspecies in Colorado.

Examination of data for Wells' plots (2172, 2180, 2190, and 2029 = respectively, my plots 22, 23, 24, and 26) lead to two conclusions:

- The Central High Plains race differed significantly from Read's Central Rockies race (Wells' 2137 and 2164 = respectively, my plots 4 and 21) and Read's Colorado Plains race (Wells' 2145 and 2155 = respectively, my plots 6 and 19) in seed weight (40 to 54 mg vs. 33 to 36 mg), foliage color in August (blue-green vs. fewer trees blue-green), foliage color in October of first growing season (green, some light purple vs. most trees light purple), foliage color in October of second growing season (gray vs. light gray to gray).
- Central High Plains differed significantly from Read's High Plains and Black Hills races (Wells' 2024, 2028, 2095, and 2197 = respectively, my plots 1, 15, 116, and 114) in seed weight (40 to 54 mg vs. 30 to 41 mg) but not in other characteristics.

---

[17] Personal communication from J.R. Haller, March 1992.

[18] Personal communication, 1992.

This taxon needs further detailed study of trees growing in situ and in provenance plantations established by Read and by Wright et al. (1969).

Smith (1977) had only one plot (= my plot 24) in the area of Central High Plains ponderosa pine. Monoterpenes in xylem oleoresins from that plot did not differ significantly from those of Rocky Mountains ponderosa pines growing nearby in either the Black Hills of South Dakota or the Front Range of Wyoming.

Southwestern Ponderosa Pine

Southwestern ponderosa pine differed significantly from both Rocky Mountains and Pacific ponderosa pine and is worthy of designation as a separate taxon. Specimens of it were collected by Wislizenus in 1846 and identified as *Pinus brachyptera* Engelmann (1848). An interesting point to note: Read's (1980) seed source 864 is nearly the same location as Wislizenus' discovery of this taxon.[19]

Read (1980, 1983) presented strong evidence for including the type location for *P. brachyptera* Engelm. in Southwestern ponderosa pine rather than in a transition zone. This pine was first collected south of Las Vegas, near what is now Romeroville, New Mexico, on the southeastern flank of the Sangre de Cristo Mountains. The cluster analysis from his seedling study would include the entire east flank of the Sangre de Cristo Mountains in Southwestern ponderosa pine. Later a cluster analysis of data from his 10-year-old plantation-grown trees indicated only the southernmost of these stands should be so included.

Read, feeling his seedling data were more meaningful, drew the northeastern bulge of Southwestern ponderosa pine to include:

- Continuous stands on the east flank of the Sangre de Cristo Mountains.
- Eight outlying stands from Romeroville north to Raton, New Mexico.
- A single stand of about 4,000 trees southeast of Kenton, Oklahoma.
- Continuous stands growing west of Trinidad, Colorado.

Smith (1977), without data from trees growing in this area, erroneously included it in his Escalante-Rio Grande transition zone. He would divide Southwestern ponderosa pine into two regions and a transition zone. Trees in his Mogollon Region had relatively high alpha-pinene (38 to 74 percent), a moderate amount of delta-3-carene (15 to 42 percent), and relatively small amounts of beta-pinene (6 to 14 percent), myrcene (5 to 15 percent), and limonene (6 to 16 percent). He also noted that xylem oleoresin in this region and his southernmost region (discussed in the next paragraph) "is typically colorless to light amber ... ." This contrasts with

---

[19] Personal communication from R.A. Read, January 30, 1992.

his observation that color of oleoresin exuding from Pacific ponderosa pine "tends toward yellow and dark amber."

Smith's smaller Coronado Region includes stands on isolated mountains in southeastern Arizona. It is based on data from only two plots. Trees from these plots had "about 90 percent alpha-pinene with small or trace amounts of the other four major components." Using data derived from a third plot, he proposed a Chiricahua Zone where slightly more delta-3-carene (12 percent vs. 1 to 2 percent) is present. He related his findings about this region and zone to findings in Peloquin's doctoral dissertation in 1971, subsequently published in 1984.

Peloquin studied cones, seeds, needles, and oleoresin from Southwestern ponderosa pine and two related species growing on six mountain ranges within Smith's Coronado Region and Chiricahua Zone. He did not find evidence for existence of either Smith's Coronado region or Chiricahua zone. Descriptors for Southwestern ponderosa pine fall almost exactly at midpoints of ranges independently established by Peloquin for Southwestern ponderosa pine. Morphological data from my three plots in southeastern Arizona plus Peloquin's nine plots do not support recognition of a different taxon either in Smith's Coronado region or his Chiricahua Zone.

Rehfeldt (1990) clearly showed strong genetic differences between his Kaibab provenance of my Southwestern ponderosa pine and his Pine Valley Mountains, Tushar Mountains, and Fishlake Plateau of my Rocky Mountains subspecies *scopulorum*. Rehfeldt (1993) demonstrated heritable differences in needle length among provenances and decreasing needle length at higher elevation within each provenance. Two of his provenances (Pinaleno Mountains and Chiricahua Mountains) were within Smith's Coronado Region and Chiricahua Zone. Rehfeldt did not recognize any differences from Southwestern ponderosa pine growing a short distance to the north. He did note that the Pinaleno Mountains' disjunct population is "so unique genetically that gene conservation programs may be desirable ... ."

Questions have been raised about my single plot from the Chisos Mountains, Big Bend National Park, southwestern Texas. The collector there was instructed to establish a plot in typical three-needled ponderosa pine, and that is what he provided. Data for plot 195 grouped without exception with data for all other plots of Southwestern ponderosa pine. Little[20] and Haller[21] both report finding three- to five-needled pines and typical *P. arizonica* in those mountains. Probably both

---

[20] Personal communication from Elbert L. Little, March 1992.

[21] Personal communication from J.R. Haller, March 1992.

species occur there, and intermediate forms may be found as well [as has been the case elsewhere in the southwest (Peloquin 1984, Rehfeldt 1993)].

All who have studied Southwestern ponderosa pine agree that it:

- Is strongly influenced by a bimodal rainfall pattern—heavy rains in both winter and summer, but dry in spring and fall
- Differs morphologically and physiologically from all other ponderosa pines.

Data from physiological research (Callaham 1959, 1962; Rehfeldt 1993) and from provenance trials—Weidman (1939), Squillace and Silen (1962), Wells (1964a), Read (1980, 1983), and Rehfeldt (1993)—support existence and uniqueness of this distinctive fast-growing taxon. The only major differences in opinion pertain to its northern limits.

Four Corners transition zone—

A very broad transition zone of morphological intergradation exists at the northern boundary of Southwestern ponderosa pine. The center of this zone led to the name "Four-Corners" transition zone. The zone's northwestern boundary starts at an undetermined point southwest of Cedar City, Utah, and extends east-northeast to Moab. Crossing into Colorado, the northeastern boundary extends east-southeast to the vicinity of Walsenburg, Colorado. Read aided in drawing the eastern boundary southward through the San Isabel National Forest and along the crest of the Sangre de Cristo Mountains. The zone's southern boundary:

- Starts a short distance southwest of Cedar City, Utah
- Turns abruptly eastward along Arizona's northern boundary to Four Corners
- Thence southeasterly it passes south of Farmington, New Mexico, and Los Alamos, New Mexico.
- Its junction with the eastern boundary is about 30 mi southeast of Santa Fe, New Mexico.

Findings of several authors support the existence and boundaries of this zone. Wells' (1964a) delineation of a less distinct southern ecotype within his central interior ecotype is almost synonymous with this transition zone in Colorado but not in Utah. Read (1980), lacking data from this region, adopted the line drawn by Wells (1964a); therefore, the southern boundary of his Central Rockies race coincides with my northeastern boundary in Colorado. The inverted V-shape of the northern boundary of this transition zone is nearly identical to the line proposed by Haller (1965) and to Smith's (1977) line delimiting the northern boundary of his Mogollon Region.

Smith's plot 46 (about 7 mi southwest of Cedar Breaks, Utah) and 50 (near South Fork, Colorado) resemble Southwestern plots. They have somewhat higher proportions of alpha-pinene and low to very low proportions of beta-pinene. Therefore, I would reposition Smith's line slightly northward to include his plots 46 and 50 in my transition zone.

Rehfeldt's (1990 and 1993) patterns of genetic variation support our drawing:

- The northwestern boundary of this transition zone to include the Markagunt, Paunsaugunt, and Aquarius Plateaus and Boulder Mountains but to exclude (as Rocky Mountains subspecies) the Tushar and Pavant Mountains and Fishlake and Wasatch Plateaus

- The northeastern boundary to include the Abajo and LaSal Mountains, Uncomphagre Plateau, and San Juan Mountains

- The southern boundary on the border between Utah and Arizona

- Its southeasterly orientation in northwestern New Mexico to include the Rio Chama watershed and Sangre de Cristo Mountains

Rehfeldt's (1990) data on growth and performance clearly placed Pine Valley Mountains (my plot 175 = Wells' 2267) in the southwestern corner of Utah within Rocky Mountains ponderosa pine; whereas, my morphological data placed it within Southwestern ponderosa pine.

This skewed diamond-shaped region is one in which powerful adaptational forces must be contributing to observed patterns of inherent variation. Northern limits of monsoonal summer rain in the southwest coincide closely with the northern boundary of this transition zone. This transition zone's southern boundary closely corresponds to the limits of southward movement of very cold continental winter storms. These dominant climatic features appear to be determinants of the Four Corners transition zone.

This transition zone seems to have significance also for bark beetles in the genus *Dendroctonus* (Smith 1977). Critchfield[22] wrote:

The genus is afflicted with a dual nomenclature due to revision by a Utah taxonomist named Wood, but it happens that species interpretations don't affect this particular problem. There are four (actually three) species of *Dendroctonus* in the southwest whose northern limits seem to be somehow related to the transition from *scopulorum* to southwestern ponderosa:

- *D. barberi* (in *brevicomis*: Wood): northern limits in southern and southwestern Colorado and southern Utah (one exception: Ashley National Forest).

_____

[22] Letter to R.A. Read, Dec. 29, 1982.

- *D. convexifrons* (in *adjunctus*: Wood): northern limits in southern Colorado (north to Rye) and southern Utah.
- *D. arizonicus* (in *frontalis*: Wood) northern limits at latitude of Flagstaff and Santa Fe (totally within the range of southwestern ponderosa pine).
- *D. approximatus* (in *parallelocollis*: Wood) northern limits at latitude of Salt Lake City and Estes Park (far north of the transition zone).

Conclusion

Morphological and climatic data lead me to conclude that ponderosa pine in Western States and adjacent Canadian provinces comprises five races deserving of subspecific taxonomic identities. Proposed subspecific epithets and races are:

- *Pinus ponderosa* subsp. *ponderosa,* Columbia ponderosa pine, southward from southern British Columbia, east of the Cascade Range in Washington, Oregon, and northeastern California and eastward to the Continental Divide.
- *Pinus ponderosa* subsp. *critchfieldiana* Callaham, subsp. *nov.,* Pacific ponderosa pine, from Puget Sound, Washington, southward to southern California.
- *Pinus ponderosa* subsp. *scopulorum* (Engelm. in S. Watson) E. Murray, Rocky Mountains ponderosa pine, from the continental divide in Montana eastward to the Black Hills of South Dakota and southward into Utah and Colorado.
- *Pinus ponderosa* subsp. *readiana* Callaham, subsp. *nov.,* central High Plains ponderosa pine, restricted to Nebraska and adjacent areas in South Dakota, Wyoming, and Colorado.
- *Pinus ponderosa* subsp. *brachyptera* (Engelm. in Wislizenus) Callaham, comb. *nov.,* Southwestern ponderosa pine, in Arizona, New Mexico, Oklahoma, and southwestern Texas, and, probably, extending into Mexico.

Four transition zones occur between subspecies:

- Helena Transition Zone
- Umpqua-Tahoe Transition Zone
- Four Corners Transition Zone
- An unnamed transition zone between ssp. *scopulorum* and ssp. *readiana*

Acknowledgments

Peter P. Feret (deceased) contributed significantly to enlargement of this manuscript while working at the Institute of Forest Genetics, Placerville, California (1983–1984) during his sabbatical leave as professor, Department of Forestry, Virginia Polytechnic Institute and State University, Blacksburg, VA 24061, USA.

Kenneth E. Diebel conducted the sophisticated discriminant statistical analyses while a post-doctoral research associate (1984), Department of Forestry, Virginia Polytechnic Institute and State University, Blacksburg, VA 24061, USA. He coauthored technical publications in 1988 and 1993.

This study was made possible, in part, by a grant from the Forest Genetics Research Foundation to the Institute of Forest Genetics, Pacific Southwest Research Station, USDA Forest Service, Placerville, California.

Metric Equivalents

When you know:	Multiply by:	To find:
Inches (in)	0.0394	Millimeters (mm)
Inches	0.394	Centimeters (cm)
Feet (ft)	3.28	Meters (m)
Miles (mi)	.621	Kilometers (km)
Acres (ac)	.405	Hectares (ha)
Milligrams (mg)	0.001	Grams (g)

Literature Cited

Baker, F.S. 1944. Mountain climates of the western United States. Ecological Monographs 14: 223–254.

Brown, M.B., ed. 1977. BMDP-77. Biomedical computer programs P-Series. Berkeley, CA: University of California Press. 880 p.

Burns, R.M., ed. 1983. Silvicultural systems for the major forest types in the United States. Agric. Handb. 445. Washington, DC: U.S. Department of Agriculture, Forest Service. 191 p.

Callaham, R.Z. 1959. *Pinus ponderosa*: geographic variation in germination response to temperature. Montreal, Canada: Proceedings, 9th International Botanical Congress: 2: 57–58.

Callaham, R.Z. 1961. Experimental taxonomy: more than seed source studies. In: Recent advances in botany, 10th International Botanical Congress. Toronto, Canada: University of Toronto Press: 1695–1699.

Callaham, R.Z. 1962. Geographic variability in growth of forest trees. In: Kozlowski, T.T., ed. Tree growth. New York: Ronald Press: 311–325.

Callaham, R.Z. 1964. Provenance research: investigation of genetic diversity associated with geography. Unasylva. 18(2-3): 40–50.

Callaham, R.Z. 2013. *Pinus ponderosa*: a taxonomic review with five subspecies in the United States. Res. Pap. PSW-RP-264. Albany, CA: U.S. Department of Agriculture, Forest Service, Pacific Southwest Research Station. 52 p.

Conkle, M.T.; Critchfield, W.B. 1988. Genetic variation and hybridization of ponderosa pine. In: Baumgartner, D.M.; Lotan, J.E., ed. Proceedings of a symposium on ponderosa pine—the species and its management. Pullman, WA: Washington State University: 27–43.

Critchfield, W.B. 1957. Geographic variation in *Pinus contorta*. Publ. 3. Cambridge, MA: Maria Moors Cabot Foundation for Botanical Research. 118 p.

Critchfield, W.B. 1984. Crossability and relationships of Washoe pine. Madroño. 31: 144–170.

Engelmann, G. 1848. Botanical appendix. In: Wislizenus, A. Memoir of a tour to northern Mexico, connected with Col. Doniphan's expedition, in 1846 and 1847. Misc. Doc. 26. Washington, DC: U.S. Senate. 89 p.

Engelmann, G. 1880. Tribe III. Abietineae. P. In: Watson, Sereno. Geological survey of California, botany. Cambridge, MA: John Wilson and Son, University Press. 2: 125–126.

Grant, M.C.; Linhart, Y. B.; Monson, R.K. 1989. Experimental studies of ponderosa pine. II. Quantitative genetics of morphological traits. American Journal of Botany. 76(7): 1033–1040.

Haller, J.R. 1962. Variation and hybridization in ponderosa and Jeffrey pine. University of California Publications in Botany. 34(2): 123–166.

Haller, J.R. 1965. The role of 2-needle fascicles in the adaptation and evolution of ponderosa pine. Brittonia. 17(4): 354–382.

Haller, J.R.; Vivrette, N.J. 2011. Ponderosa pine revisited. Aliso. 29(1): 53–57.

Hartley, H.O.; Rao, J.N.K.; LaMotte, L. 1978. A simple synthesis-based method variance component estimation. Biometrics. 34: 233–242.

Klecka, W.R. 1980. Discriminant analysis, Sage University paper series on quantitative applications in the social sciences. Beverly Hills, CA: Sage Publications.

Korstian, C.L. 1924. A silvical comparison of the Pacific coast and Rocky Mountain forms of western yellow pine. American Journal of Botany. 11: 318–324.

Linhart, Y.B.; Grant, M.C.; Montazer, P. 1989. Experimental studies in ponderosa pine. I. Relationship between variation in proteins and morphology. American Journal of Botany. 76(7): 1024–1032.

Little, E.L., Jr. 1979. Checklist of United States trees (native and naturalized). Agric. Handb. 541. Washington, DC: U.S. Department of Agriculture. 375 p.

Mason, H. L.; Stockwell, P. 1945. A new pine from Mount Rose, Nevada. Madroño. 8(2): 61–63.

Milligan, G.W. 1980. An examination of the effect of six types of error perturbation on fifteen clustering algorithms. Psychometrika. 45: 325–342.

Monson, R.K.; Grant, M.C. 1989. Experimental studies of ponderosa pine. III. Differences in photosynthesis, stomatal conductance, and water-use efficiency between two genetic lines. American Journal of Botany. 76(7): 1041–1047.

Murray, E. 1982. *Notae Spermatophytae*. Kalmia. 12: 23.

Niebling, C.R.; Conkle, M.T. 1990. Diversity of Washoe pine and comparisons with allozymes of ponderosa pine races. Canadian Journal of Forest Research. 20: 298–308.

Peloquin, R.L. 1984. The identification of three-species hybrids in the ponderosa pine complex. The Southwestern Naturalist. 29(1): 115–122.

Perry, J.P., Jr. 1991. The pines of Mexico and Central America. Portland, OR: Timber Press. 231 p.

Rao, C.R. 1973. Linear statistical inference and its application. New York: John Wiley and Sons. 522 p.

Ray, A.A., ed. 1982. SAS user's guide: statistics, 1982. Cary, NC: SAS Institute. 584 p.

Read, R.A. 1980. Genetic variation in seedling progeny of ponderosa pine provenances. Forest Science Monograph 23. 59 p.

Read, R.A. 1983. Ten-year performance of ponderosa pine provenances in the Great Plains of North America. Res. Pap. RM-RP-250. Fort Collins, CO: U.S. Department of Agriculture, Forest Service, Rocky Mountain Research Station. 17 p.

Rehfeldt, G.E. 1986a. Adaptive variation in *Pinus ponderosa* from Intermountain regions. I. Middle Columbia River system. Res. Pap. INT-RP-373. Ogden, UT: U.S. Department of Agriculture, Forest Service, Intermountain Research Station. 9 p.

Rehfeldt, G.E. 1986b. Adaptive variation in *Pinus ponderosa* from Intermountain regions. II. Snake and Salmon River basins. Forest Science. 32: 79–92.

Rehfeldt, G.E. 1990. Genetic differentiation among populations of *Pinus ponderosa* from the upper Colorado River basin. Botanical Gazette. 151: 125–137.

Rehfeldt, G. E. 1991. Models of genetic variation for *Pinus ponderosa* in the inland Northwest (U.S.A.). Canadian Journal of Forest Research. 21: 1491–1500.

Rehfeldt, G.E. 1993. Genetic variation in the Ponderosae of the Southwest. American Journal of Botany. 80: 330–343.

Smith, R.H. 1977. Monoterpenes of ponderosa pine xylem resin in western United States. Tech. Bull. 1532. Washington, DC: U.S. Department of Agriculture, Forest Service. 48 p.

Smith, R.H. 1981. Variation in immature cone color of ponderosa pine (Pinaceae) in northern California and southern Oregon. Madroño. 28: 272–275.

Smith, R.H. 2000. Xylem monoterpenes of pines: distribution, variation, genetics, function. Gen. Tech. Rep. PSW-GTR-177. Albany, CA: U.S. Department of Agriculture, Forest Service, Pacific Southwest Research Station. 454 p.

Sorenson, F.C. 1994. Genetic variation and seed transfer guidelines for ponderosa pine in central Oregon. Res. Pap. PNW-RP-472. Portland, OR: U.S. Department of Agriculture, Forest Service, Pacific Northwest Research Station. 24 p.

Squillace, A.E.; Silen, R.R. 1962. Racial variation in ponderosa pine. Forest Science Monograph 2. 27 p.

Sturgeon, K.B. 1979. Monoterpene variation in ponderosa pine xylem resin related to western pine beetle predation. Evolution. 33(3): 803–814.

U.S. Weather Bureau. 1954. Climatic summary of the United States—supplement for 1931 through 1952. Climatography of the United States 11—(various numbers corresponding to individual states). Washington, DC: U.S. Department of Commerce.

Weidman, R.H. 1939. Evidences of racial influence in a 25-year test of ponderosa pine. Journal of Agricultural Research. 59(12): 855–887.

Wells, O.O. 1964a. Geographic variation in ponderosa pine. I. The ecotypes and their distribution. Silvae Genetica. 13(4): 89–103.

Wells, O.O. 1964b. Geographic variation in ponderosa pine. II. Correlations between progeny performance and characteristics of the native habitat. Silvae Genetica. 13(5): 125–132.

Wright, J.W.; Lemmien, W.A.; Bright, J.N. 1969. Early growth of ponderosa pine ecotypes in Michigan. Forest Science. 15(2): 121–129.

Federal Recycling Program
Printed on Recycled Paper